AF815667

QUE Bee

From Doubts to Distinction

Your ISC 2027 Exams Partner

GIST OF THE TEXTBOOK

Crisp & Complete Theory - No need to go back to bulky textbooks!

ALL TYPES OF LATEST PATTERN QUESTIONS

MCQs | Case-based | Assertion-Reason; All in one place!

KEYWORDS HIGHLIGHTED

Important points and key words are neatly highlighted; Never miss what matters

PICTURE-BASED QUESTIONS

Questions based on identifying events, monuments or scenes from a given picture

COUNCIL-STYLE ANSWERS

Write responses like an examiner expects

SAMPLE PAPER

Practice in real-exam mode. Perfect your timing, strategy and confidence.

Study Smart, Score Higher

ARIHANT PRAKASHAN
(School Division Series)

卐 **ADMINISTRATIVE & PRODUCTION OFFICES**

Regd. Office
'Ramchhaya' 4577/15, Agarwal Road, Darya Ganj, New Delhi -110002
Tele: 011- 47630600, 43518550; Fax: 011- 23280316

卐 **Head Office**
Kalindi, TP Nagar, Meerut (UP) - 250002, Tel: 0121-7156203, 7156204

卐 **SALES & SUPPORT OFFICES**
Agra, Ahmedabad, Bengaluru, Bareilly, Chennai, Delhi, Guwahati, Hyderabad, Jaipur, Jhansi, Kolkata, Lucknow, Nagpur & Pune.

PO No : TXT-59-T070224-4-26

Published By Arihant Publications (India) Ltd.

For further information about the books published by Arihant, log on to www.arihantbooks.com or e-mail at info@arihantbooks.com

Follow us on

卐 **PRICE** ₹175.00

PRODUCTION TEAM

Publishing Manager
Keshav Mohan

Category Head
Karishma Yadav

Project Head
Shivam Gupta

Cover Designer
Bilal Hashmi

Inner Designer
Ankit Tyagi

Page Layouting
Amit Dev

Proof Reader
Priya Kumari

QUE Bee

ISC History Class 11

Types of Questions & their Respective Number

Type of Questions	Total Number
Multiple Choice Questions (MCQs)	123
Assertion-Reason (A-R)	53
Very Short Answer Questions (VSA)	105
Short Answer Type Questions (SA)	74
Long Answer Type Questions (LA)	40
TOTAL NO. OF QUESTIONS	**395**

Ace Your ISC Exams with Confidence!

Created by

Anubhuti Thakur

B.Ed.

8 Yrs. Experienced

Nachiketa Higher Secondary School

Contributor

Divya Gupta

QUE Bee

LEARNING PATH

Your Complete Study direction at a glance...

LATEST COURSE STRUCTURE

Updated as per the latest curriculum guidelines...

There will be two papers in the subject:
Paper I: Theory 3 hours ------ 80 marks
Paper II: Project Work --------20 marks

INDIAN HISTORY

1. Emergence of the Colonial Economy

(i) Development of the means of transport and communication.
Transportation: a brief look at the development of the railways.

(ii) Effect of British revenue policy:
Impact on peasants and artisans
Disruption of the traditional economy.
A general account of the impact of the British revenue policies on peasants and artisans.

(iii) Development of modern industries.
An account of the growth of large-scale machine based industries in Western India, its economic impact.

(iv) Colonial Forest Policy - impact on local communities.
An overview of the 19th century Colonial Forest Policy. Political and economic impact of the Colonial Forest Policy on local communities.

2. Social Movements

(i) Struggle against caste – Jyotirao Phule, Narayan Guru, Veerasalingam.
A brief outline of their contributions to Indian society.

(ii) The Women's Question
Women's condition in India in the 19th century. Features of the following Acts: Abolition of Sati (1829), Widow Remarriage (1856), Female Infanticide Prevention (1870) and Age of Consent (1891) - their impact on Indian women.

3. Protest Movements against Colonial Rule

Circumstances that led to different protest movements: the Indigo Uprising (1859), Deccan riots (1875), Munda Uprising (1899-1900) and the impact on the colonial policies.

4. Growth of Nationalism

(i) Swadeshi Movement
Partition of Bengal and anti-Partition Movement including the Swadeshi and Boycott Movement: causes and impact of the movement.

(ii) Foundation of the Muslim League.
Circumstances leading to its foundation.
Objectives of the Muslim League.

5. Gandhian Nationalism (1916 – 1922)

(i) Agitation against the Rowlatt Act, Jallianwala Bagh (1919).
The reasons behind the Rowlatt Act and its main terms to be studied in brief. A general account of the satyagraha against the Act, leading to Jallianwala Bagh.

(ii) The launching of the passive resistance movement by Gandhi: Khilafat and Non-Cooperation Movement (1919-1922).
The launching of the Khilafat and the Non-Cooperation Movements. There should be a connected chronological account of both the movements and their suspension.

LATEST COURSE STRUCTURE

6. Gandhian Nationalism (1927 – 1937)

(i) Lahore session and declaration of 'Poorna Swaraj' as the Congress objective.

Events leading to the Lahore session – Simon Commission: a brief explanation of the reasons for its boycott; demand for Dominion Status by 1929 (Nehru Report).

The main points of the Poorna Swaraj Resolution.

(ii) Civil Disobedience Movement (1930-1934).

A general account of the features of the Movement; main terms of the Gandhi-Irwin Pact; the 1st and 2nd Round Table Conferences; resumption of the Movement and the Poona Pact.

(iii) Government of India Act, 1935.

The main features of Government of India Act, 1935 should be explained.

A critical account of the election of 1937. A summary of the main developments under Congress and non-Congress ministries should be included.

WORLD HISTORY

7. World War I: Causes, events leading to it; Peace settlements

(i) Main long-term causes: alliance system, imperialism, militarism (arms race), nationalism.

Main short-term causes: events from 1908 to 1914.

(ii) Paris Peace Settlements-Changes in the map of Europe; critical evaluation of the Treaty of Versailles.

8. The Great Depression

(i) Causes leading to the Wall Street Crash of 1929 and its impact on the economy of USA, Germany & Japan.

(ii) Roosevelt and the New Deal – (a) Aims (b) Measures taken.

9. Rise of Communism under Stalin in Russia (1917 -1939)

(i) The Russian Revolution of 1917 - causes of the March Revolution and its results; weaknesses of the Provisional Government leading to the November Revolution.

(ii) Lenin: reasons for New Economic Policy (NEP) and its impact.

(iii) Rise of Stalin to power and factors assisting his rise.

(iv) Main features of Stalin's domestic policy: Collectivisation of agriculture.

Industrialisation: First and Second Five Year Plans Purges of 1937-1938.

10. Rise of Fascism under Mussolini in Italy (1919-39)

(i) Post-War discontent and the rise to power of Benito Mussolini.

Conditions which gave rise to Fascism; a brief chronological account of the events which brought Mussolini to power from the election of 1921 to the march on Rome in October 1922.

(ii) Main features of Mussolini's domestic policy.

Critical appraisal of Mussolini's policies particularly his economic policy.

11. Rise of Nazism under Hitler in Germany (1933-39)

(i) Rise of Hitler to power and factors assisting his rise.

Weaknesses of the Weimar Republic as a background to the rise of Nazism; events from 1932 onwards leading to Hitler becoming Chancellor of Germany in 1933; the reasons for his popularity among different groups should be explained.

(ii) The Nazi State: from 1933 onwards.

Outline of the changes made by Hitler in government, the cultural life and education, army (the Night of the Long Knives), the economy and religious life. Escalation of the campaign against the Jews should be done in some detail, till the "Final Solution". Reasons why his policies were accepted among different groups.

12. Rise of Militarism in Japan (1919-37)

Reasons for the rise of militarism in the 1930s.

GENERAL GUIDELINES FOR History EXAMINATION

As per Council for the Indian School Certificate Examinations (CISCE)

1. Avoid **selective study**; prepare all topics thoroughly.
2. Develop a chronological understanding using timelines and flowcharts.
3. Learn and internalise **cause-effect relationships**, especially for wars and political movements.
4. Prepare structured notes covering background, causes, course, implications, outcomes, and significance.
5. Practice writing concise, structured answers with clear introductions and conclusions.
6. Use headings, subheadings, bullets, and underline keywords in answers.
7. Familiarise yourself with key terms, acronyms, and their full forms.
8. Refer to multiple authenticated sources, such as history books by different authors, relevant documentaries, speeches, and visuals on each topic.
9. **Understand visuals** (cartoons, posters, maps) through regular interpretation practice.
10. Cultivate **curiosity-driven learning** by exploring the reasons behind events.
11. Practice past papers in a time-bound manner.
12. Maintain clear presentation and logical sequencing in answers (follow the question order).
13. Avoid unnecessary elaboration and focus on qualitative, relevant points.
14. Prepare mind maps and summary tables for each topic.
15. Align answers with mark allocation.

16. Build exam readiness through regular revision and confidencebuilding.
17. Avoid last-minute cramming; focus on spaced and active revision.
18. Ensure clarity when writing question numbers and chosen options.
19. Enhance answer writing by improving coherence, clarity, and overall prose.
20. Practice regularly using **Analysis of Pupil Performance** of ISC
21. History, competency-focused practice questions, and latest specimen papers for better framing of answers.

Indian History

1

EMERGENCE OF THE COLONIAL ECONOMY

- A colonial economy is an economic system in which a controlling power exploits the resources, labour and markets of a colony for its own benefit.
- In India, the British reorganised the economy to serve their industrial, financial and imperial interests. This change caused economic exploitation, slow growth and long-term poverty in India.

Development of the Means of Transport and Communication

- In the early years of British rule, the East India Company paid little attention to the development of transport and communication.
- After the Industrial Revolution, the demand for raw materials from India increased, which prompted the need for better transport facilities.
- British merchants required improved transport facilities to move raw materials from the interior regions to ports.
- Roads, river routes, and later railways were developed mainly to serve British economic and military interests.
- Lord William Bentinck started road-building programmes, including a " Grand Trunk road" connecting Calcutta with the United Provinces.
- The Public Works Department (PWD) was established to construct and maintain roads, canals, and railways.

Lord William Bentinck

Development of Railways

- The railways were introduced in India by the British to serve their economic, administrative and military needs.
- Lord Dalhousie played an important role in the expansion of the railway network in India and he is also known as the "Father of Indian Railways".
- The first railway line in India was opened in 1853 between Bombay and Thane.
- Railways helped in carrying raw materials and goods from the interior of India to ports for export to Britain.
- Railway construction was mainly financed by British capital under the Guarantee System. Under this system, British investors were assured a fixed return of 5 percent on their investment and were given land free of cost.
- The colonial administration in India compensated companies for any losses, which placed a heavy financial burden on India.
- The Guarantee System was abolished in 1873 because of criticism. But it was reintroduced in 1888 with a lower rate of interest.
- On the recommendation of the Acworth committee, railway construction finally came under direct control of government.

Lord Dalhousie

Objectives of the Growth of Railways

- One major objective of railway expansion was the fast and cost effective transportation of raw materials to ports for export.
- Railways helped in the easy distribution of British manufactured goods across Indian markets.
- Another important objective was the swift movement of British troops to suppress revolts and maintain control.

Expansion of Railways under British rule in India

Impact of Railways

Negative Impact

- The railways were constructed under the Guarantee System, which ensured fixed profits (usually 5%) to British investors.
- Indian revenues were used to cover losses, while profits were sent to Britain.
- Indians were heavily taxed to bear the cost of railway construction.
- Indian traders and passengers faced discrimination in railway services.
- Railways did not promote industrial growth in India because engines, coaches and spare parts were imported from England.
- Karl Marx remarked that 'the railways were useless to Hindus'.

Positive Impact

- The railway network improved connectivity between different regions of India.
- It contributed to Nation-building or social solidarity by bringing people closer.
- Railways helped spread ideas of nationalism among the educated middle class.

British Revenue Policies and their Effect

- After acquiring the Diwani Rights in 1765, the British aimed to maximise land revenue.
- Land revenue became the main source of income for the British administration.
- To achieve this goal, three major land revenue systems were introduced.

Land Revenue Systems

Permanent Settlement | Ryotwari Settlement | Mahalwari Settlement

Permanent Settlement (1793)

Lord Cornwallis

- It was also known as 'Sunset Law'. If revenue was not paid by sunset on specific day, the zamindari was auctioned off.
- The Permanent Settlement was introduced by Lord Cornwallis in Bengal, Bihar and Orissa.
- Under this system, zamindars were recognised as the owners of land.
- Zamindars were required to pay a fixed amount of revenue to the British government.
- This system led to the exploitation of peasants through high rents.
- It resulted in the rise of absentee landlords who showed little interest in agricultural improvement.

Ryotwari Settlement

Sir Thomas Munro

- The Ryotwari system was introduced by Sir Thomas Munro in parts of South and Western India.
- Under this system, land revenue was collected directly from the peasants, known as ryots.
- Peasants were not given permanent rights over land.
- High revenue demands pushed many peasants into poverty and indebtedness.

Mahalwari Settlement

Holt Mackenzie

- The Mahalwari system was introduced by Holt Mackenzie in North-Western India.
- Under this system, land revenue was collected from entire village communities, known as mahals.
- Although villages were treated as revenue units, heavy taxation caused financial hardship among peasants.

Impact of British Revenue Policies on Peasants

- Peasants were burdened with heavy land revenue demands. They were exploited by zamindars, moneylenders and government officials.
- Excessive taxation and lack of agricultural support led to frequent famines.
- Many peasants lost their land and became deeply indebted.

Impact of British Revenue Policies on Artisans

- British economic policies favoured machine-made goods imported from England.
- Indian handicrafts and textile industries lost both domestic and international markets.
- Heavy import duties were imposed on Indian goods entering England.
- British goods entered Indian markets at very low tariffs.
- Large-scale de-industrialisation led to unemployment among artisans. Many artisans were forced to migrate to rural areas to take up agriculture.

Disruption of the Traditional Economy

- India was transformed from an exporter of finished goods into a supplier of raw materials.
- Traditional industries collapsed under British economic policies.
- The Indian economy became dependent on British industrial needs.
- A continuous drain of wealth occurred *via* profits, salaries, pensions, and home charges.
- This drain of wealth severely weakened India's economic structure.

Development of Modern Industries

Growth of Large-Scale Machine-Based Industries in Western India

- The British introduced modern industries in India mainly to serve their own economic interests.
- British capitalists invested heavily in railways, plantations, mining and a few selected industries.
- India provided favourable conditions such as cheap raw materials, abundant labour and banking facilities. As a result, large-scale machine-based industries developed mainly in Western India.
- Indian communities like the Parsis and Gujaratis played a significant role in the growth of these industries.

Dadabhai Naoroji

R.C. Dutt

- Bengalis were largely excluded from industrial opportunities, while Marwaris acted as intermediaries between British firms and Indian markets.

Economic Impact

- Industrial development in India was limited and uneven across regions. Most industries remained dependent on British capital, machinery and technology.
- Profits earned from Indian industries were largely sent back to Britain.
- Colonial policies discouraged the growth of independent indigenous industries.
- Dadabhai Naoroji and R.C. Dutt criticised the British economic policy.

Colonial Forest Policy

- Forests were freely used by local communities for fuel, fodder and grazing before British rule. The British introduced scientific forestry to serve their imperial and commercial needs.
- In 1855, Lord Dalhousie issued the Charter of Indian Forests, which marked the beginning of systematic forest policy.
- Dietrich Brandis was appointed the first Inspector General of Forests in 1856.
- The Indian Forest Act of 1865 established legal control over forests.
- The Forest Act of 1878 further restricted access by classifying forests into three categories i.e. Reserved Forest, Protected Forest and Village Forest.

Dietrich Brandis

Political and Economic Impact on Local Communities

- Traditional rights of forest-dwelling communities were taken away.
- Local people were denied access to essential forest resources such as fuel, fodder and minor forest produce.
- Forest policies primarily served British interests, such as providing timber for railways and shipbuilding.
- Protests by local communities were largely ignored, which caused hardship and resentment.

EXAM ORIENTED QUESTIONS

TYPE - 1   1 Mark

Multiple Choice Questions

Q.1 He is often referred to as the 'Father of Indian Railways'□for actively promoting railway construction in India during British rule. Identify the Governor-General described above.

(a) Lord William Bentinck
(b) Lord Dalhousie
(c) Lord Cornwallis
(d) Lord Hardinge

Ans. (b) Lord Dalhousie

Q.2 Which outcome from railway construction is cited as a social benefit that indirectly aided the growth of nationalism?

(a) A rapid increase in rural employment and wage levels.
(b) Immediate industrial development of village economies.
(c) Greater mobility of people and circulation of ideas across different regions of India.
(d) The removal of economic and travel discrimination in railway services.

Ans. (c) Greater mobility of people and circulation of ideas across different regions of India.

Q.3 Which statement BEST captures a major economic criticism of the railway guarantee system?

(a) It prevented any foreign investment in India.
(b) It ensured all railway profits stayed in India.
(c) It encouraged profit repatriation to Britain while Indians bore costs.
(d) It made rail travel free for Indian passengers.

Ans. (c) It encouraged profit repatriation to Britain while Indians bore costs.

Q.4 Which of the following was a direct administrative outcome of Lord Dalhousie's□emphasis on public works?

(a) Abolition of the P.W.D.
(b) Creation of a Central Public Works Department and provincial branches.
(c) Immediate Indianisation of railway senior posts.
(d) Complete withdrawal of British capital from infrastructure.

Ans. (b) Creation of a Central Public Works Department and provincial branches.

Q.5 Which of the following BEST summarises why the Acworth Commission's□recommendation mattered for railways?

(a) It increased the guaranteed interest to 7%.
(b) It led to abolition of the guarantee system and greater government control over railways.
(c) It nationalised all jute mills.
(d) It transferred P.W.D. duties to private companies.

Ans. (b) It led to abolition of the guarantee system and greater government control over railways.

Q.6 The following is a picture of a 19th-century scene showing a steam engine at a Calcutta river bank and it was being loaded with sacks of jute.

Which of the following factors BEST explains why British merchants pressed the East India Company to develop transport and communication networks in India?

(a) Railways were constructed mainly to encourage Indian handicrafts.
(b) Railways and ports facilitated the export of raw materials such as jute to Britain.
(c) Jute cultivation declined as a result of railway expansion.
(d) Indian-owned companies controlled most jute mills and retained profits within India.

Ans. (b) Railways and ports facilitated the export of raw materials such as jute to Britain.

Q.7 Which British Governor-General gave special attention to improving river navigation between Calcutta and Assam to support tea plantations and transport?

(a) Lord Dalhousie
(b) Lord Cornwallis
(c) Lord William Bentinck
(d) Lord Hardinge

Ans. (c) Lord William Bentinck

Q.8 Which of the following land revenue systems introduced by the British had an objective similar to eliminating intermediaries by establishing a direct relationship between the state and cultivators in parts of the Madras and Bombay Presidencies?

(a) Permanent Settlement, which fixed land revenue permanently with zamindars.

(b) Mahalwari Settlement, which assessed revenue collectively from village communities.

(c) Ryotwari Settlement, which collected revenue directly from individual cultivators (ryots).

(d) Zamindari Settlement, where revenue was mediated through landlords.

Ans. (c) Ryotwari Settlement, which collected revenue directly from individual cultivators (ryots).

Q.9 Identify the key social outcome of the Permanent Settlement introduced by the British in India.

(a) It immediately strengthened land ownership rights of peasants.

(b) It led to the emergence of absentee zamindars who frequently exploited peasants.

(c) It resulted in the rapid industrial revival of textile centres like Dacca.

(d) It ensured the universal grant of pattas to all cultivators.

Ans. (b) It led to the emergence of absentee zamindars who frequently exploited peasants.

Q.10 Which act allowed the government to acquire private land for public purposes and also affected forest areas during British rule?

(a) Indian Forest Act, 1865

(b) Land Acquisition Act, 1894

(c) Indian Forest Act, 1878

(d) Land Acquisition Act, 1890

Ans. (b) Land Acquisition Act, 1894

Q.11 Identify the act described below.

It reorganised forests into Reserved, Protected, and Village categories, strengthened government control, and restricted the traditional rights of local communities.

(a) Charter of Indian Forests, 1855

(b) Land Acquisition Act, 1894

(c) Indian Forest Act, 1878

(d) Forest Conservation Act, 1927

Ans. (c) Indian Forest Act, 1878

Q.12 The extract given below explains how British economic policies transformed India into a colony supplying raw materials while exploiting peasants, artisans, forests, and industries for imperial interests.

Which of the following consequences of the colonial economy can be directly applied to explain this transformation?

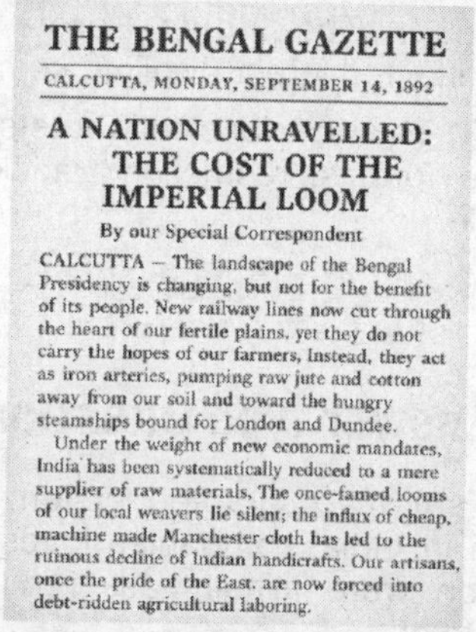

THE BENGAL GAZETTE

CALCUTTA, MONDAY, SEPTEMBER 14, 1892

A NATION UNRAVELLED: THE COST OF THE IMPERIAL LOOM

By our Special Correspondent

CALCUTTA – The landscape of the Bengal Presidency is changing, but not for the benefit of its people. New railway lines now cut through the heart of our fertile plains, yet they do not carry the hopes of our farmers, Instead, they act as iron arteries, pumping raw jute and cotton away from our soil and toward the hungry steamships bound for London and Dundee.

Under the weight of new economic mandates, India has been systematically reduced to a mere supplier of raw materials, The once-famed looms of our local weavers lie silent; the influx of cheap, machine made Manchester cloth has led to the ruinous decline of Indian handicrafts. Our artisans, once the pride of the East, are now forced into debt-ridden agricultural laboring.

P : Conversion of India into a supplier of raw materials for British industries.

Q : Decline of Indian handicrafts due to the influx of British manufactured goods.

R : Growth of self-reliant indigenous industries across India.

S : Drain of wealth from India to Britain through profits and revenue.

Options

(a) P and Q (b) R and S (c) P, Q and S (d) Q and R

Ans. (c) P, Q and S

Assertion-Reason Questions

Given below are two statements marked as Assertion (A) and Reason (R). Read the two statements and select the correct option from the codes given below.

Codes

(a) Both A and R are true and R is the correct explanation of A.

(b) Both A and R are true, but R is not the correct explanation of A.

(c) A is true, but R is false.

(d) Both A and R are false.

Q.1 Assertion (A) The railway guarantee system imposed a heavy financial burden on India.

Reason (R) British investors were assured fixed profits, while the Indian government compensated railway companies for losses.

Ans. (a) Both A and R are true and R is the correct explanation of A.

Q.2 Assertion (A) The Permanent Settlement fixed the land revenue permanently in 1793.

Reason (R) Cornwallis believed granting zamindars hereditary ownership would encourage them to invest in land improvements.

Ans. (b) Both A and R are true, but R is not the correct explanation of A.

Q.3 Assertion (A) The Indian Forest Act of 1878 adversely affected forest-dwelling communities.

Reason (R) The Act classified forests into reserved and village forests, restricting traditional rights of local people.

Ans. (a) Both A and R are true and R is the correct explanation of A.

Very Short Answer Type Questions

Q.1 Under the railway guarantee system introduced by the British in India, companies investing in railway construction were initially assured a guaranteed interest rate of ....

Ans. 5 percent

Q.2 British merchants during colonial rule emphasised the need for improved transport facilities in India. State one reason why British merchants advocated for improved transport in India.

Ans. They wanted quicker movement of raw materials from the interior regions to ports and easy distribution of British manufactured goods in Indian markets.

Q.3 Expand PWD.

Ans. Public Works Department

Q.4 The image given below shows the cover page of a book written by an Indian economist criticising British economic policies in India.

Name the author of the book who highlighted the drain of wealth from India to Britain.

Ans. Dadabhai Naoroji

Q.5 Refer to the image given below and name the author that criticised British economic policies in India.

Ans. R.C. Dutt

Q.6 In the picture shown below, ... can be seen inspecting the construction of railway lines in India, whose vision and administrative efforts greatly expanded the railway network to serve British economic, administrative, and military interests.

Ans. Lord Dalhousie

Q.7 British economic policies in colonial India opened Indian markets to cheap British machine-made goods while imposing high duties on Indian manufactures. What was the significance of these policies for Indian artisans and the textile industry?

Ans. These policies led to the deindustrialisation of Indian textiles, causing widespread unemployment among artisans and forcing many to shift to agriculture for survival.

Q.8 Mention any one merit of railways introduced in colonial India.

Ans. One merit was that railways linked different provinces and promoted a sense of national unity by enabling easier travel and communication.

Q.9 Name one community in Western India that led native industrial growth in cotton mills.

Ans. The Parsi community played a leading role in establishing cotton mills in Western India.

TYPE - 2 — 4 Marks

Short Answer Type Questions

Q.1 With reference to the historical account given below, state any four reasons why the East India Company initially neglected the development of transport and communication in India.

THE FREE PRESS JOURNAL

EAST INDIA PEOPLE SHOUT FOR INDIA

FIFTY.EICT TUDAY

Thirong te casty ride in Indie the fivoriulle Company alleplayed litlls iawrerp lq tanprowing the tomejpn and conmmaication unfrasmncture.

East India Company Neglects Transport Development

Dithting lis catly rute in Untla, the East lindis company enggrupad bille listeraltral anprasting flis subacorinent's framport and communication prisetanmdlts

The Company achmristnation was, propstraphan thhs reqronding is. twenmqval Bntontion, numiore collection and fearaiung be uadie nuvooly.

The refloting vesils and after ceniies vnure laugliti/igogmcil, leading Inimulan ditreome andnenathong fos trootent trowement of goods and people

Elliorts to invest an tollnes, and and other lnainonrgatters anh exerged lutar anwen by marmienal pressorls from Brillasi nacecnnnifants.

TOOIAW HE OMINS FLME DERTLE MELES -BIST ONGE..

Ans. The East India company neglected the development of transport and communication in India due to the following reasons

- The Company was mainly focused on its territorial expansion and political power.
- Its primary aim was to earn profits through trade and land revenue, not to improve infrastructure as it is costly overhead.
- Roads and communication networks were not considered essential during the initial phase of British administration.
- Investment in transport only began later due to pressure from British merchants and the need to move raw materials, goods, and troops efficiently.

Q.2 The British government introduced railways in India during the 19th century as a key measure to strengthen its economic and political control over the colony. The report highlights that railway expansion was closely connected with imperial trade requirements, facilitating the movement of raw materials for export, and with military administration, enabling the rapid deployment of British troops across different regions of India.

Source: The Times of India (Archive)

Based on the above report, state any four reasons why the East India Company agreed to open railways in India.

Ans. The East India company agreed to open railways in india for the following reasons

- Railways were needed to transport raw materials such as cotton, jute, coal and tea quickly from the interior regions to ports for export to Britain.
- They helped in the easy and wide distribution of British machine-made goods to Indian markets, including villages.
- Railways enabled the British government to move troops rapidly to suppress revolts and maintain political control over India.
- They also strengthened administrative control by improving communication between major cities, military centres and ports.

Q.3 "Improvement of Transportation and communication system helped the growth of Indian nationalism." Do you agree? Give reasons.

Ans. The improvement of transportation and communication system helped in the growth of Indian Nationalism by the following reasons

- Railways, roads, and river steamers allowed people from different regions to travel and interact more easily for exchanging ideas.
- Newspapers and postal services helped nationalists spread their ideas and reach a wider audiences.
- Students and intellectuals could attend educational institutions in other provinces, creating awareness about colonial exploitation.
- Improved transport made it easier to organise protests, rallies, and political meetings, strengthening unity and national consciousness.

Q.4 The graph below shows the impact of British revenue policies and agricultural output during the 18th - 19th centuries on the Indian peasantry.

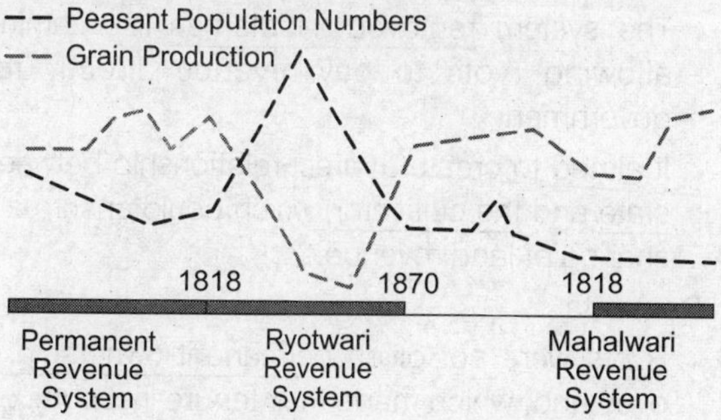

With reference to the above graph, explain the main features of the Permanent, Ryotwari and Mahalwari revenue systems. Why did these systems lead to widespread hardship among peasants as reflected in the chart?

Ans. Features of Revenue Systems

- **Permanent Settlement (1793)** Zamindars were recognised as landowners and required to pay fixed revenue to the British government; peasants had to pay high rents.
- **Ryotwari System** Revenue was collected directly from individual cultivators (ryots); peasants had no permanent ownership, and high taxes pushed them into poverty.
- **Mahalwari System** Land revenue was assessed collectively from village communities (mahals); heavy taxation caused financial stress for entire villages communities.

Reasons for Hardship Reflected in the Chart

- Excessive revenue demands forced peasants to borrow from moneylenders, increasing indebtedness which often led to confiscation of land and property.

Q.5 The Ryotwari Settlement was introduced by the British in parts of South and Western India, under which land revenue was collected directly from the peasants without the involvement of intermediaries. However, the system also imposed heavy revenue demands and did not grant permanent ownership rights to the cultivators.

In the above context, analyse two merits and two demerits of the Ryotwari Settlement.

Ans. The Ryotwari Settlement was a land revenue system introduced by the British in parts of South and Western India, where the government collected revenue directly from the cultivators.

Merits

- The system removed middleman like zamindars, allowing ryots to pay revenue directly to the government.
- It aimed to create a direct relationship between the state and the cultivator, which could ensure a fairer sharing of land revenue.

Demerits

- Ryots were not given permanent ownership rights over land, which made their tenure insecure.
- Heavy revenue rates and strict collection methods caused poverty and hardship among peasants.
- Revenue was not fixed, it was revised every 20-30 years, often resulting in steep increases.

Q.6 State any four reasons to explain how British revenue and economic policies adversely affected Indian peasants and artisans during colonial rule.

Ans. British revenue and economic policies were designed to serve imperial interests rather than Indian welfare. These policies deeply affected both peasants and artisans by destroying traditional livelihoods and increasing economic hardship.

- Heavy land revenue demands forced peasants into indebtedness and made farming unprofitable.
- Zamindars, moneylenders and British officials exploited peasants under the revenue systems.
- British policies favoured these cheap machine-made goods from England, destroying the Indian handicrafts industry.
- Large-scale deindustrialisation caused unemployment among artisans, forcing many to shift to agriculture.

Q.7 State any two reasons for the deindustrialisation of India after the Industrial Revolution in Britain. Mention any two effects of this process on Indian artisans and traditional industries.

Ans. Reasons for Deindustrialisation

(i) Indian markets were opened to cheap machine-made British goods, reducing the demand for local products.

(ii) High duties and restrictions on Indian goods exported to Britain limited the foreign market opportunities for these goods.

Effects of Artisans and Traditional Industries

(i) Indian artisans and weavers lost their traditional livelihoods, leading to widespread unemployment.

(ii)Traditional industries declined and many workers were forced to shift to agriculture or other low-paying jobs over-burdening of agriculture.

Q.8 State any two reasons why large-scale machine-based industries developed mainly in Western India. Mention any two groups that played a role in their growth.

Ans. Large-Scale Industries developed in Western India because of the following reasons

(i) Western India had abundant and cost effective raw materials for industrial use.

(ii) Labour was plentiful, and banking facilities supported industrial investments.

Groups Involved

(i) The Parsee community played a major role in establishing cotton mills.

(ii) The Gujarati community actively participated in trade and industrial growth.

Q.9 **State any two factors that made India attractive for British industrial investment. Mention any two communities that were excluded or acted as intermediaries in these industries.**

Ans. Factors Attracting Investment

(i) Cheap raw materials were available in India.

(ii) Labour was abundant and inexpensive.

Communities Involved or Excluded

(i) Bengalis were largely excluded from industrial opportunities.

(ii) Marwaris acted as intermediaries or middleman between British firms and Indian markets.

Q.10 **State any two negative economic impacts of modern industries introduced by the British in India. Mention any two reasons why these industries remained dependent on British control.**

Ans. While modern industries were established in India, most were controlled by British capital and primarily served colonial interests, causing several economic drawbacks.

Negative Impacts

(i) Profits earned from Indian industries were largely sent back to Britain.

(ii) Independent indigenous industries were discouraged from growing.

Reasons for Dependence

(i) Most industries relied on British machinery and technology.

(ii) British capital financed the industries, keeping Indians dependent on foreign control.

Q.11 **Identify the personality given in the picture. Discuss any two of his contributions in critiquing British economic policies. Mention any two impacts of his work on Indian economic thought.**

Ans. The personality in the picture is 'Dadabhai Naoroji'. He was one of the earliest Indian economic critics of British colonial rule who analysed how British policies drained wealth from India.

Contributions of Dadabhai Naoroji

(i) He formulated the Drain of Wealth theory, showing how British rule systematically transferred India's wealth to Britain without an adequate return.

(ii) Naoroji highlighted these ideas in his book Poverty and Un-British Rule in India, explaining how colonial economic policies impoverished India.

Impacts of His Work on Indian Economics

(i) His critique helped Indian nationalists understand and challenge British economic exploitation.

(ii) It provided an intellectual foundation for economic nationalism and later movements against British rule.

Q.12 **Discuss any two contributions of R.C. Dutt in analysing British colonial economic impact. Mention any two outcomes of his work for Indian society.**

Ans. Contributions of R.C. Dutt

(i) In The Economic History of India, he documented how British taxation and land revenue systems devastated Indian agriculture and rural economies.

(ii) Dutt also explained how British policies led to the gradual decline of India's handloom and indigenous industries, turning India into a supplier of raw materials and a market for British manufactured goods.

Outcomes of His Work

(i) His work helped Indians realise the economic roots of colonial exploitation and poverty.

(ii) It strengthened economic arguments within the freedom movement, motivating Indians to demand self-rule and industrial revival

TYPE - 3 8 Marks

Long Answer Type Questions

Q.1 Discuss the impact of railways on Indian society and economy during British rule.

Ans. The impact of railway on Indian society and economy during British rule were as follows

- The railways were constructed under the Guarantee System, which assured fixed profits to British investors regardless of actual earnings.
- Any losses incurred by railway companies were paid from Indian revenue, while profits were transferred to Britain, increasing the drain of wealth.
- Indians were heavily taxed to meet the high cost of railway construction and maintenance.
- Indian traders and passengers often faced discrimination in fares, freight charges, and railway services.
- Railway development did not encourage Indian industrial growth because engines, coaches, and spare parts were imported from England.
- Despite these drawbacks, railways improved connectivity by linking distant regions of India through a common transport network.
- They contributed to national integration by enabling people from different regions, cultures, and communities to travel and interact more easily.
- Railways also helped in the spreading ideas of nationalism, especially among the educated middle class, by facilitating communication and exchange of political ideas.

Q.2 Explain how the British land revenue policies led to the exploitation of peasants and contributed to the disruption of the traditional Indian economy during colonial rule.

Ans. British land revenue policies led to the exploitation of peasants and contributed to the disruption of the traditional Indian economy during colonial rule in the following ways

- The British made land revenue the primary source of income, imposing heavy financial burdens on peasants.
- Under the Permanent Settlement, zamindars were recognised as landowners and often charged high rents, exploiting the peasants.
- In the Ryotwari system, peasants (ryots) paid revenue directly to the government but lacked permanent ownership of land, leaving them insecure.
- The Mahalwari system assessed revenue from entire village community, which caused financial hardship due to heavy taxation.
- Excessive revenue demands forced peasants into debt and poverty, often resulting in the loss of their land.
- Lack of agricultural support and high taxes contributed to frequent famines.
- British economic policies promoted the export of raw materials and import of British machine-made goods, undermining traditional industries.
- The continuous drain of wealth, including profits, salaries, and pensions, weakened the economic structure of India and disrupted its self-sustaining traditional economy.

Q.3 With reference to the British rule in India.

(a) State any four factors that contributed to the growth of industries in Western India.

(b) Discuss any four economic impacts of these industries on India under British rule.

Ans. (a) Factors contributing to industrial growth in Western India

(i) British capitalists invested heavily in railways, plantations, mining and selected industries.

(ii) The region had cheap raw materials and abundant labour, which encouraged large-scale industrial activity.

(iii) Communities such as the Parsis and Gujaratis actively participated in establishing and managing industries.

(iv) Marwaris acted as intermediaries, linking British firms with Indian markets, facilitating trade and investment.

(b) Economic impacts of industrial growth

(i) Industrial development was limited and uneven across India, with western India benefiting more than other regions.

(ii) Most industries remained dependent on British capital, machinery and technology, restricting local industrial autonomy.

(iii) Profits from Indian industries were largely sent back to Britain, creating a drain of wealth from India.

(iv) Independent Indian industries were discouraged, and critics like Dadabhai Naoroji and R.C. Dutt highlighted the exploitative nature of British economic policies.

Q.4 Before British rule, forests were freely used by local communities, but colonial policies drastically restricted access to them.

(a) Identify any two laws introduced by the British to regulate forests in India. State key features of these laws.

(b) Discuss any four political and economic impacts of colonial forest policies on local communities.

Ans. (a) Laws introduced and their features

(i) **The Charter of Indian Forests 1855** marked the beginning of systematic forest management.

(ii) **The Indian Forest Act, 1878** classified forests into Reserved, Protected and Village forests; restricted access of locals; served British commercial interests.

(b) Political and economic impacts on local communities

(i) Traditional rights of forest-dwelling communities, such as collection of fuel, fodder and minor forest produce were taken away.

(ii) Local people were denied access to essential forest resources for their daily livelihood.

(iii) Forest policies primarily served British interests, such as providing timber for railways and shipbuilding.

(iv) Protests by local communities were largely ignored, leading to hardship, resentment and social tension.

2

SOCIAL MOVEMENTS

- Indian society witnessed several social reform movements during the 19th century.
- These movements aimed to challenge social evils such as caste discrimination, gender inequality and oppressive customs.

Struggle Against Caste

- The caste system divided Indian society and treated lower castes as inferior.
- Many reformers strongly opposed this discrimination and worked for social equality.

Jyotirao Phule (1827-1890)

Jyotirao Phule

- Jyotirao Phule was the prominent social reformer from Maharashtra. He strongly criticised the caste system and the dominance of Brahmins in society.
- He worked for the upliftment of lower castes and backward communities. In Maharashtra he is known as 'Mahatma Phule'.

Contributions

- Jyotirao Phule promoted female education by opening a girls' school in Poona in 1851, with the active support of his wife Savitribai Phule.
- He worked for the education of the depressed classes and established schools for children from lower castes who were denied learning opportunities.
- Phule launched a strong movement against untouchability and urged lower castes to reject Brahmin dominance and perform their own religious rituals.
- In 1873, he founded the Satya Shodhak Samaj, which became a powerful organisation to fight caste oppression and promote social equality.
- He criticised the Indian National Congress for neglecting the cause of the repression and wrote influential works like *Dharma Tritiya Ratna* and *Life of Shivaji* to inspire social reform.

Sri Narayana Guru (1855-1928)

Sri Narayana Guru

- Sri Narayana Guru was a spiritual leader and social reformer from Kerala. He belonged to the Ezhava community, which was considered a lower caste.

Contributions

- Sri Narayana Guru founded the Sree Narayana Dharma Paripalana Yogam (SNDP), which became a major movement for the upliftment of the depressed classes in Kerala.
- He worked to end untouchability, especially against castes lower than that of the Ezhavas and gave them dignity and social recognition.
- He built temples open to all castes, breaking the monopoly of Brahmins over religious worship and rituals.

- He simplified religious rituals and declared that complicated Mantras were invented by Brahmins to maintain their dominance.
- He preached the ideal of "One caste, one religion, one God", which emphasised social equality and unity.
- His movement compelled the government to recognise the Ezhavas as a backward class entitled to protection in jobs and education.

Kandukuri Veeresalingam (1848-1919)

- Kandukuri Veeresalingam was a social reformer from Andhra Pradesh. He opposed caste discrimination and outdated social customs.

Kandukuri Veeresalingam

Contributions

- Veeresalingam was a pioneer of social reform in Andhra. He strongly advocated widow remarriage and arranged the first widow remarriage in 1881 despite violent opposition from orthodox leaders.
- He promoted women's education and established girls' schools in Rajamundry in 1874 and 1884 to encourage literacy and empowerment among women.
- He founded the Hitakarini Society and donated all his property to support social activities aimed at improving society.
- He was a prolific writer. He was the first Telugu novelist, the first to write a History of Telugu poets, and the first to translate scientific works into Telugu.
- He earned the title of Father of modern Telugu literature.
- He was deeply influenced by Brahmo Samaj leaders like Raja Ram Mohan Roy and Vidyasagar, and in 1887, he established the first Brahma Mandir at Rajamundry.
- He played a role in the national movement and served as a member of the first Indian National Congress session in 1885, and was honoured with the title 'Rao Bahadur' in 1893 for his reformist contributions.

The Women's Question

Women's Condition in India in the 19th century

- In the 19th century, women suffered from many social evils such as Sati, child marriage, widow oppression and female infanticide (killing of a female infant).
- Women were subjected to the inhuman practice of Sati, where widows were burnt alive on their husband's funeral pyres.
- Child marriage was widespread, which forced girls into marriage at a very young age, often before puberty.
- Widows lived very difficult lives. They were not allowed to remarry and were forced to live alone and faced social neglect and suffering.
- Women were largely denied education and orthodox society opposed female literacy and restricted their intellectual growth.
- Women were treated as subordinate and dependent and their lives dictated by rigid customs and patriarchal norms.
- Reformers highlighted that women's condition symbolised the stagnation of Indian society and made their upliftment essential for social progress.

Abolition of Sati (1829)

- Muslim rulers such as Muhammad bin Tughluq, Akbar and Jahangir along with Sikh Gurus, Maratha leaders and even European powers had prohibited Sati in their territories.
- Missionaries like William Carey and the Serampore Group studied Hindu scriptures and argued that Sati was not compulsory.They submitted memorials and urged for its abolition.
- Mritunjoy Vidyalankar was a Sanskrit scholar who stated that the practice of Sati had no support in the scriptures and was not compulsory. His views later influenced and strengthened the arguments of social reformers.

- Raja Ram Mohan Roy emerged as a leading figure in the anti-Sati movement. He organised vigilance groups to stop the practice at the cremation grounds. He published pamphlets in 1818, 1819 and 1829 in which he opposed Sati.
- In his journal Sambad Kaumudi along with missionary newspapers like Samachar Darpan, Raja Ram Mohan Roy supported the abolition of Sati.
- Conservative leaders like Raja Radha Kanta Deb, defended Sati and wrote Samachar Chandrika in favour of Sati and mobilised petitions against reform.
- Governor-General Lord William Bentinck, passed Regulation XVII of 1829 and declared Sati illegal and punishable by criminal courts.

Impact of the Abolition of Sati

- The practice of Sati was legally ended and thousands of women's lives were saved.
- It marked the beginning of government intervention in social reforms and women's rights began to receive public attention.

Widow Remarriage Act (1856)

- In the early 19th century, attempts to introduce widow remarriage were initiated by Raja Rajballabh of Dacca. These efforts failed due to strong opposition from conservative rulers.
- The movement gained strength when Pandit Ishwar Chandra Vidyasagar took up the issue. He wrote a pamphlet in 1855 using ancient scriptures (Shastras) to prove that widow remarriage was permitted.
- Petitions that supported widow remarriage were submitted to the Legislative Council by prominent leaders of Bengal, including the Maharaja of Burdwan and several zamindars.
- With the initiative of J. P. Grant, the government passed Act XV of 1856, which legalised widow remarriage in India.

Impact of the Widow Remarriage Act

- Social discrimination against widows slowly reduced and widows received legal permission to remarry.
- The act encouraged further reforms for women and promoted the idea of dignity and equality for widows.

Female Infanticide Prevention Act (1870)

- Female infanticide was the practice of killing female infants soon after birth.
- In the 19th century, female infanticide was widely practiced in Bengal, Orissa and parts of Western India, especially among communities such as the Jats, Ahirs and Gurjars, largely due to the heavy burden of dowry.
- The British Parliament took notice of the problem and detailed reports on infanticide were presented in the House of Commons in 1824 and 1828.
- After investigation, the government passed the Female Infanticide Prevention Act in 1870, which aimed to curb this social evil.
- The act empowered authorities to take measures in specific districts, make rules, punish offenders and place neglected children under supervision.
- This act was mainly enforced in the North-Western Provinces, which included Awadh, Agra, and Punjab. In these regions, the entire Pargana region were sometimes declared 'blood red' to identify areas where infanticide was widely practiced.

Impact of the Female Infanticide Prevention Act

- The act strengthened legal protection for girls and helped to spread awareness about the importance and value of girl children.
- It encouraged society to rethink gender discrimination.
- Although the act had only partial success due to resistance from dominant landed classes, it was a significant step in legally addressing the crime and protecting the lives of female children.

Age of Consent Act (1891)

- In 1860, the first law against child marriage prohibited marriage for Hindu girls below ten years of age, but the issue remained unresolved.
- The reformer Behramji Malabari played a key role against child marriage. He wrote pamphlets in 1884, known as Malabari's Notes, in which he exposed the negative effects of infant marriage and widowhood while suggesting as increase in the age of consent.
- His efforts drew wide attention among officials and reformers, leading to the proposal of a new law to raise the age of consent from 10 to 12 years.
- The Age of Consent Bill was passed in 1891. The conservatives viewed it as foreign interference in Hindu customs, while reformers and groups like the Brahmo Samaj supported it.
- Leaders such as Bal Gangadhar Tilak and orthodox journals like Kesari and Mahratta opposed the Bill and argued that it endangered Hindu traditions. On the other hand, reformers defended it as necessary for protecting child wives.

Impact of the Age of Consent Act

- The Act marked an important step toward women's rights and social reform, and increased public debate on child marriage.
- It marked progress toward social reform and gender justice, and girls received a significant legal protection against exploitation.

REVISION NOTES

EXAM ORIENTED QUESTIONS

TYPE - 1

1 Mark

Multiple Choice Questions

Q.1 "Jyotirao Phule founded an organisation to direct his anti-Brahmin movement and to work for the upliftment of women and the downtrodden sections of society." Identify the organisation founded by Jyotirao Phule to fight caste oppression.

(a) Brahmo Samaj (b) Satya Shodhak Samaj
(c) Arya Samaj (d) Hitakarini Society

Ans. (b) Satya Shodhak Samaj

Q.2 The following is a picture of Mahatma Jyotirao Phule, a pioneer social reformer of Maharashtra in the 19th century.

Which one of the following best describes the focus of Jyotirao Phule's social reform activities?

(a) Promotion of political nationalism and self-rule.
(b) Reform of religious rituals within Hinduism.
(c) Upliftment of women and the downtrodden sections through social reform.
(d) Expansion of British-supported educational institutions.

Ans. (c) Upliftment of women and the downtrodden sections through social reform.

Q.3 "Narayana Guru's social reform movement challenged untouchability and demanded equal social rights, which ultimately compelled the government to grant protective recognition to a specific community."

Which of the following communities was recognised as a backward class as a result of Narayana Guru's movement?

(a) Rajputs (b) Ezhavas
(c) Ahirs (d) Gurjars

Ans. (b) Ezhavas

Q.4 Who among the following social reformers of Kerala is remembered for the slogan "One caste, one religion, one God for mankind"?

(a) Raja Ram Mohan Roy
(b) Swami Dayanand Saraswati
(c) Narayana Guru
(d) Kandukuri Veeresalingam

Ans. (c) Narayana Guru

Q.5 Which of the following actions of Kandukuri Veeresalingam is similar in objective to the reforms carried out by Sri Narayana Guru ?

(a) Supporting the monopoly of Brahmins over religious rituals.
(b) Promoting social equality by challenging caste discrimination and outdated customs.
(c) Opposing education for women and lower castes.
(d) Encouraging blind obedience to traditional social practices.

Ans. (b) Promoting social equality by challenging caste discrimination and outdated customs.

Q.6 Who was conferred the title 'Rao Bahadur' in 1893?

(a) Jyotirao Phule (b) Narayana Guru
(c) Veeresalingam (d) Vidyasagar

Ans. (c) Veeresalingam

Q.7 Identify the social reformer who organised vigilance groups to prevent the practice of Sati cremation grounds.

(a) Lord William Bentinck
(b) Raja Ram Mohan Roy
(c) William Carey
(d) Ishwar Chandra Vidyasagar

Ans. (b) Raja Ram Mohan Roy

Q.8 Identify the key difference between the role of Raja Ram Mohan Roy and conservative leaders like Raja Radha Kanta Deb in the debate on Sati.

(a) Raja Ram Mohan Roy supported Sati, while conservative leaders opposed it.
(b) Raja Ram Mohan Roy used journals and pamphlets to argue for abolition, while conservative leaders defended Sati through petitions and newspapers.
(c) Conservative leaders worked with missionaries to abolish Sati, while Raja Ram Mohan Roy opposed foreign intervention.
(d) Raja Ram Mohan Roy played no role in the movement, while conservative leaders led the abolition campaign.

Ans. (b) Raja Ram Mohan Roy used journals and pamphlets to argue for abolition, while conservative leaders defended Sati through petitions and newspapers.

Q.9 The extract given above discusses social reformers who opposed caste discrimination, untouchability, and Brahmin dominance, and worked to promote social equality through education, religious reform, and social organisations. *(Source: www.thenews.com)*

The Struggle for Social Equality

The extract discusses social reformers who opposed caste discrimination, untouchability

Equality for all

Breaking caste barriers

Breaking caste barriers

Legacy of justice

These reformers challenged sociall norms, and laid for the foundation for a more equally India, embracing the step to education social justice, and religious reform.

Legacy of justice

Kandukuri Veesalingam played a key figure in Andhra Pradesh a social reformer advocated widow remarriage and promoting female education by founding the Hitakarini Society to advance discrimination and inequality.

Which of the following actions best reflects the common objective of these reformers?

P : Opening schools only for boys and lower-caste children

Q : Establishing organisations to challenge caste oppression

R : Supporting the monopoly of Brahmins over religious rituals

S : Promoting social equality and dignity for depressed classes

(a) P and R (b) Q and S (c) P and Q (d) R and S

Ans. (b) Q and S

Q.10 Identify who among the following reformers wrote pamphlets on Widow Remarriage in 1855?

(a) Jyotirao Phule (b) Veeresalingam

(c) Vidyasagar (d) Malabari

Ans. (c) Vidyasagar

Assertion-Reason Questions

Given below are two statements marked as Assertion (A) and Reason (R). Read the two statements and choose the corrects answer from the codes given below.

Codes

(a) Both A and R are true and R is the correct explanation for A.

(b) Both A and R are true, but R is not the correct explanation for A.

(c) A is false, but R is True.

(d) A is true, but R is false.

Q.1 **Assertion** (A) Sri Narayana Guru's reform movement immediately ended caste discrimination in Kerala.

Reason (R) His movement led the government to recognise the Ezhavas as a backward class entitled to protection in jobs and education.

Ans. (c) A is false, but R is True.

Q.2 **Assertion** (A) The Widow Remarriage Act completely eliminated social opposition to remarriage in India.

Reason (R) Although the act allowed wid remarriage legally, the practice remained rare due to social stigma.

Ans. (c) A is false, but R is True.

Q.3 **Assertion** (A) The Female Infanticide Prevention Act of 1870 aimed to curb the killing of girl children.

Reason (R) The act gave authorities power to punish offenders, enforce rules and supervise neglected children in affected regions.

Ans. (a) Both A and R are true and R is the correct explanation for A.

Very Short Answer Type Questions

Q.1 The image given below shows the cover page of the book 'Dharma Tritiya Ratna'.

Name the social reformer who authored this book and worked for the upliftment of lower castes and promotion of women's education.

Ans. Jyotirao Phule

Q.2 Expand SNDP.

Ans. Sree Narayana Dharma Paripalana Yogam (SNDP)

Q.3 Kandukuri Veeresalingam established the .... to support social activities and improve society.

Ans. Hitakarini Society

Q.4 Refer to the image given below and name the organisation that Veeresalingam established in Rajamundry.

Ans. Brahma Mandir

With the initiative of J. P. Grant, the government passed Act XV of 1856, which legally allowed widow remarriage in India."

(Source: Widow Remarriage Act, 1856)

State any one impact of the Widow Remarriage Act of 1856 on Hindu society.

Ans. The act legally permitted widows to remarry, which helped reduce social stigma against widows and promoted dignity and equality for women.

Q.6 .... wrote the Malabari's Notes on infant marriage?

Ans. Behramji Malabari

Q.7 The Age of Consent Act was passed in 1891 to raise the minimum age of consummation of marriage for Hindu girls from ten to twelve years.

What was the significance of this act in the context of women's rights?

Ans. It provided legal protection to child wives, initiated public debate on child marriage, and marked progress toward social reform and gender justice.

TYPE - 2 4 Marks

Short Answer Type Questions

Q.1 Jyotirao Phule strongly opposed caste discrimination and worked for the upliftment of lower castes and women's education in 19th-century India.

In the above context, analyse the impact of Jyotirao Phule's efforts on social equality and education in India.

Ans. Jyotirao Phule's efforts had a significant impact on society, these are as follows

- He promoted female education by opening a girls' school in Poona in 1851, which encouraged literacy and empowerment among women.
- He worked for the education of children from lower castes and it helped in the upliftment of marginalised communities.
- He promoted social equality and questioned the rigid caste hierarchy by challenging untouchability and Brahmin dominance.
- He established the Satya Shodhak Samaj, which became a platform to fight caste oppression and inspired social reform and awareness across India.

Q.2 State any four contributions of Brahmo Samaj in social and educational reform.

Ans. The four contributions of Brahmo Samaj in social and educational reform are as follows

(i) The Brahmo Samaj strongly opposed social evils such as Sati, child marriage, polygamy and caste discrimination, and worked to purify Hindu society.

(ii) Leaders like Raja Ram Mohan Roy and later Brahmo reformers encouraged widow remarriage while fighting against the rigid restrictions imposed on widows.

(iii) The Brahmo Samaj established schools and colleges, promoted English education, and encouraged women's education, thereby contributing to the modernisation of Indian society.

(iv) It simplified religious practices, rejected idol worship, and emphasised monotheism, while also promoting social equality and rational thinking.

Q.3 Discuss any four contributions of Veeresalingam Kandukuri to justify why he is regarded as the prophet of modern Andhra.

Ans. Contributions of Veeresalingam Kandukuri are as follows

(i) Veeresalingam Kandukuri was a great champion of widow remarriage. He established a Remarriage Association and arranged the first widow remarriage in Rajahmundry on 11th December, 1881.

(ii) He strongly promoted female education, founding a girls' school in 1874 and another in 1884, at Rajahmundry, encouraging women's empowerment.

(iii) He established the Hitakarini Society and donated all his property to support social activities aimed at improving society.

(iv) Veeresalingam was a pioneer in Telugu literature; he became the first Telugu novelist, the first to write a history of Telugu poets and the first to translate scientific works into Telugu, laying the foundation of modern Andhra society.

Q.4 Lord William Bentick,the then Governor - General of British India passed the famous Regulation XVII in1829 that deemed Sati as illegal and punishable by courts.

Raja Ram Mohan Roy warmly advocated the introduction of Western education in India. And thus he became a pioneer of English Education in India and of Enlightened journalism in his country.

Source : International Journal of Humanities, Art and Social Studies.

Based on the above report, state any four reasons that led to the abolition of Sati in India.

Ans. Four reasons that led to the abolition of Sati in India are as follows

(i) The extreme cruelty and injustice of Sati, which caused the deaths of numerous widows, created widespread moral outrage and convinced reformers and the government to act.

(ii) Missionaries like William Carey and the Serampore group studied Hindu scriptures and proved that Sati was not compulsory, urging its abolition.

(iii) Sanskrit scholar Mritunjoy Vidyalankar stated that Sati had no scriptural support, which reinforced arguments for its abolition.

(iv) Growing public awareness and strong campaigns by social reformers highlighted the injustice of Sati, pressuring the government to intervene.

Q.5 With reference to the extract given below, state any four contributions of Behramji Malabari in the movement against child marriage in India.

Source: scalar.lehigh.edu

25, Hornby Road,

Bombay, *15th August, 1884.*

Dear Sir,

I beg to submit for your consideration my Notes on Infant Marriage and Enforced Widowhood in India.

There cannot be two opinions as to the existence of the evils and their disastrous effects. The question is how best to mitigate these, without calling in the aid of direct legislation and witithout offending the susceptibilities of the orthodox.

I have ventured to make a few suggestions in these papers, and trust that, in your turn, you will not fail to advance the cause by giving me the benefit of your practical experience. I submitted these Notes some time ago to prominent members of the Government of India, and am much encouraged by their sympathy and their readiness to do everything in their power, on proper representation, conistently with the declared policy of the British Government in this country.

I have no right to count upon your entire approval of these views—all that I hope for is that you will not set them aside as impracticable or unworthy of consideration.

Yours respectfully,

BEHRAMJI M. MALABARI.

Ans. Behramji Malabari played a key role in bringing attention to the evils of child marriage and improving the status of girls in India. His four contributions were as follows

(i) In 1884, Behramji Malabari wrote two important pamphlets on infant marriage and the hardships of widowhood. These became well known as Malabari's Notes.

(ii) He sent these Notes to leading officials in India and also to prominent people in England. This helped draw wide attention to the social problems of child marriage and enforced widowhood.

(iii) Malabari suggested changes to the Hindu Marriage Act asking that the age of consent for girls be raised from ten to twelve years.

(iv) His efforts played a key role in the passing of the Age of Consent Act of 1891, which made it illegal to consummate a marriage before the wife had reached the age of twelve.

TYPE - 3 8 Marks

Long Answer Type Questions

Q.1 Narayana Guru declared, "One caste, one religion, one God."

(a) Identify the movement started by Narayana Guru. State any three aims of this movement.

(b) Discuss any four contributions of Narayana Guru in the field of social reform in Kerala.

Ans. (a) The movement started by Narayana Guru was the Sree Narayana Dharma Paripalana (SNDP) Movement.

Three aims of this movement were

(i) To discard untouchability and promote equality among all castes.

(ii) To build temples and open them to people of all castes, high or low.

(iii) To simplify Brahmanical rituals and free the society from priestly monopoly.

(b) Four contributions of Narayana Guru in the field of social reform in Kerala are as follows

(i) Narayana Guru built temples that were open to all castes, thereby breaking caste barriers.

(ii) He simplified religious rituals for puja, marriage, and funerals and made them accessible to ordinary people.

(iii) He emphasised education and social unity, which encouraged the upliftment of the Ezhava community and other depressed classes.

(iv) His slogan "One caste, one religion, one God" became a powerful call for social equality and harmony in Kerala.

Q.2 "In 1855, Ishwar Chandra Vidyasagar wrote a pamphlet quoting verses from the Hindu Shastras to prove that widow remarriage was permissible."

With reference to the above source, explain Vidyasagar's role in the passing of the Widow Remarriage Act and its subsequent impact on Indian society.

Ans. Vidyasagar's role in the passing of the Widow Remarriage Act and its subsequent impact on Indian society are as follows

Vidyasagar's Role

- Ishwar Chandra Vidyasagar was deeply moved by the miserable condition of Hindu widows. In 1855, he wrote a pamphlet based on authoritative verses from the Shastras and argued strongly in favour of widow remarriage.
- He mobilised public opinion by submitting petitions to the Legislative Council, supported by the Maharaja of Burdwan and several zamindars.
- Despite strong opposition from the orthodox Hindus led by Raja Radha Kanta Deb, Vidyasagar remained firm in his mission.
- With the initiative of J.P. Grant, the Widow Remarriage Act (Act XV of 1856) was passed, legalising widow remarriage in India.

Impact on Society

- The Act gave legal sanction to widow remarriage, though in practice it remained rare due to social resistance.
- It marked a significant step in reforming Hindu society and inspired similar movements in Punjab (by Arya Samaj) and Western India.
- The Act highlighted the growing role of reformers and the colonial government in challenging orthodox practices.
- It laid the foundation for future reforms aimed at improving the status of women in Indian society.

Q.3 **Discuss any eight features of the Female Infanticide Prevention Act of 1870.**

Ans. The features of the Female Infanticide Prevention Act of 1870 are as follows

(i) The act empowered the government to take special measures in districts where female infanticide was prevalent.

(ii) It authorised officials to frame rules and regulations to prevent the practice.

(iii) These rules had to be confirmed and published by the government for enforcement.

(iv) The court prescribed punishments for breach of rules, making offenders legally liable under the law.

(v) It allowed the government to place neglected children under supervision to ensure their safety.

(vi) The act provided for the continuation savings of prosecutions under other laws, meaning offenders could be punished under multiple legal provisions.

(vii) It clearly defined the extent of the act, applying it mainly to the North-Western Provinces including Awadh, Agra and Punjab.

(viii) The act was coercively enforced in certain areas, with whole Parganas publicly proclaimed 'blood-red' to mark them as guilty of infanticide.

3

PROTEST MOVEMENTS AGAINST COLONIAL RULE

- During British colonial rule, peasants and tribal communities in India faced severe exploitation.
- The British land revenue systems, moneylenders and planters forced cultivators into poverty and misery. As a result, several protest movements arose in different regions of India.
- The most important protest movements were the Indigo Uprising (1859), the Deccan Riots (1875) and the Munda Uprising (1899-1900).
- These movements revealed the suffering of peasants and tribals and forced the colonial government to make changes in its policies.

Indigo Uprising (1859)

Circumstances

- Indigo was in great demand in Europe as a dye for colouring cotton fabrics produced in factories.
- Many retired army officers and planters, who had migrated from America, started indigo plantations in Bengal and Bihar.
- Peasants were forced to grow indigo instead of food crops like paddy and wheat, which led to hunger and misery in their families.
- Planters cheated peasants by measuring land unfairly (2 1/2 bighas counted as 1 bigha) and forced them to sign exploitative contracts.
- The planters paid advances and then forced peasants to sell indigo at the lowest rates.

Indigo Revolt

- Those who resisted were tortured, confined in indigo factories without food or water, their houses were attacked and women were dishonoured.
- Local officials and courts supported European planters, while native judges were not allowed to punish European offenders and left peasants helpless.

Protest

- Peasants first sent mass petitions to the government, but these were ignored.
- Leaders like Digambar and Vishnu Charan Biswas of Nadia district organised a boycott of indigo cultivation and encouraged peasants to remain firm despite torture and false lawsuits.
- Peasants carried out largely non-violent protests they refused to sow indigo and even went to prison voluntarily.
- Harish Chandra Mukerjee, the editor of Hindu Patriot, wrote bold articles filled with facts and data against planter tyranny.
- Dinabandhu Mitra wrote the play composed a Bengali drama named Nil Darpan, in which he portrayed the suffering of peasants.

Harish Chandra Mukerjee

REVISION NOTES

- The play was translated into English by Michael Madhusudan Dutta and published by Bishop James Long, who was fined rupees 1000. The fine was paid by Kali Prasanna Sinha, who was an enlightened zamindar.
- The play and articles stirred public opinion in Bengal and created sympathy for the peasants.

Nil Darpan by Dinabandhu Mitra

Impact on Colonial Policies

- Governor Grant was worried by the situation and he remembered the Santhal Rebellion. He issued a proclamation stating that no peasant could be forced to grow indigo against his will.
- The government appointed the Indigo Commission to record complaints of peasants and planters.
- Following the Commission's recommendations, the government stated that ryots were free to refuse indigo cultivation, which significantly reduced the planters control over the peasants in Bengal. This corrective step limited the power of the planters, forcing them to shift their plantations from Bengal to Bihar and Uttar Pradesh.

Deccan Riots (1875)

Circumstances

- The Deccan region was mainly dependent on cotton cultivation.
- Peasants, especially the Kunbis borrowed money from local moneylenders (mahajans) at very high interest rates to meet cultivation expenses.
- In 1870, the price of cotton suddenly fell in the international market.
- Peasants who had invested heavily in cotton cultivation could not repay their loans.
- Moneylenders seized their lands and immovable property and transferred ownership from peasants to their own names. This exploitation created widespread anger among the peasants.

Deccan Riot

Protest

- Peasants first tried to socially boycott moneylenders. When this failed, they rose in revolt in Poona and Ahmadnagar districts.
- Peasants attacked the houses of moneylenders, burnt debt records and destroyed property.
- The revolt was led by Kenglia; however, his subsequent arrest broke the morale of the rebels.
- In Bombay province, the Ramosi tribal peasants also revolted against zamindars and moneylenders but their movement was suppressed by the British army.
- The Koya Rebellion took place in the Eastern Godavari region of present-day Andhra Pradesh. It was led by Tomma Dora, who was regarded as the king of Malkangiri. The rebellion came to an end after Tomma Dora was shot dead by the police.

Impact on Colonial Policies

- The colonial government passed the Deccan Agriculturists' Relief Act (1879) to protect the interests of peasants.
- The act restricted the power of moneylenders by regulating loans, especially those involving the mortgage of land and property. It made the registration of contracts, bonds, and mortgages compulsory in government offices to ensure transparency and legal protection for peasants.
- The act also provided legal safeguards to prevent unfair seizure of land and property by moneylenders.

Tomma Dora

Munda Uprising

Circumstances

- The Mundas were an ancient tribal community living in Chhota Nagpur (Ranchi and Hazaribagh).
- Their traditional land system was called Khunt-Katti, which means collective ownership of land.
- British land revenue policies destroyed this system and imposed high taxes and encouraged landlords and moneylenders to exploit the Mundas.
- The community lost its customary rights over forest land and faced forced labour.
- Initially, the missionaries were supported by the Mundas community. Later, the Mundas felt disappointed when the missionaries tried to convert them to Christianity, which led to resentment and dissatisfaction against colonial officers, zamindars, moneylenders, and even missionaries.

Protest

- Birsa Munda was the son of a poor peasant, who emerged as the leader of the movement.
- He declared that land belonged to the Mundas and called for liberation from British control.
- Birsa was arrested and jailed in 1895, but after his release, he issued a call to destroy all oppressors.
- The Mundas attacked police stations, churches, and government offices with traditional weapons like bows, arrows and axes. The Mundas gave heroic resistance to colonial authority.
- Consequently, the movement was suppressed and Birsa was arrested again and died in jail in 1900. Many Mundas were executed or sent to the Andaman jail.

Birsa Munda

Impact on Colonial Policies

- The colonial administration recognised and restored the Khunt-Katti system, which acknowledged the traditional collective ownership of land by tribal communities.
- Laws were enacted to restrict the transfer of tribal land to non-tribals (dikus), and provided some protection against exploitation by moneylenders, landlords and traders.

EXAM ORIENTED QUESTIONS

TYPE - 1   1 Mark

Multiple Choice Questions

Q.1 During the 19th century, a natural dye produced in India became extremely popular in European factories. This demand led European planters to establish plantations in eastern India, forcing peasants to grow the crop under oppressive conditions.□

Identify the primary reason for the high demand for this crop in Europe.

(a) It was used for colouring cotton fabrics
(b) It was used in making medicines
(c) It was used in paper production
(d) It was used in shipbuilding

Ans. (a) It was used for colouring cotton fabrics

Q.2 During the Indigo Uprising, two local leaders from the Nadia district played a crucial role in organising peasants and leading the boycott of indigo cultivation.

Who among the following were these leaders of the Indigo peasants in Nadia district?

(a) Harish Chandra Mukerjee and Dinabandhu Mitra
(b) Digambar and Vishnu Charan Biswas
(c) Bishop James Long and Kali Prasanna Sinha
(d) Michael Madhusudan Dutta and John Baptist

Ans. (b) Digambar and Vishnu Charan Biswas

Q.3 One literary work played a crucial role in exposing the oppression and cruelty faced by peasants under the indigo planters and helped shape public opinion against planters tyranny.

Which of the following dramas most effectively exposed the tyranny of the indigo planters?

(a) Neel Chitra (b) Nil Darpan
(c) Neel Aasman (d) Nill Varnan

Ans. (b) Nil Darpan

Q.4 Which of the following best explains why the Deccan region's of economy made peasants vulnerable to the 1875 revolt?

(a) The region's dependence on cotton made peasants highly sensitive to international price fluctuations.
(b) The British forcibly imposed rice cultivation, which peasants resisted.
(c) Peasants refused to borrow money from moneylenders, creating cash shortages.
(d) Indigo production collapsed due to famine and drought.

Ans. (a) The region's dependence on cotton made peasants highly sensitive to international price fluctuations.

Q.5 The extract given below is on a report of Deccan Riot. Which of the following measures were introduced by the British to safeguard peasants after the Deccan Riots?

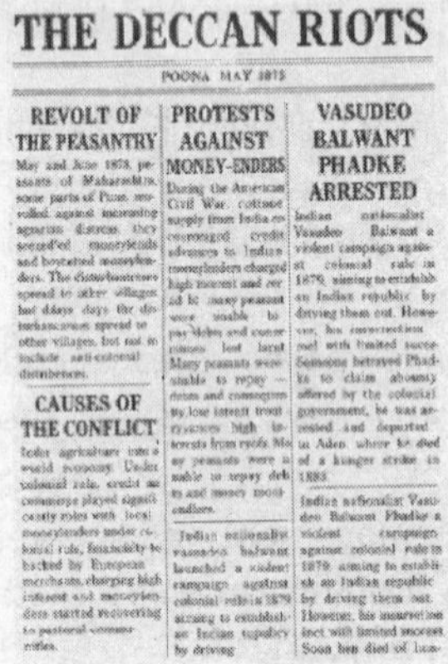
THE DECCAN RIOTS

POONA MAY 1875

REVOLT OF THE PEASANTRY

CAUSES OF THE CONFLICT

PROTESTS AGAINST MONEY-ENDERS

VASUDEO BALWANT PHADKE ARRESTED

P : Restriction on the sale of land for the recovery of debt
Q : Registration of contracts and mortgages in government offices
R : Abolition of indigo cultivation
S : Provision of free seeds for cotton cultivation

(a) P and S (b) Q and R (c) P and Q (d) R and S

Ans. (c) P and Q

Q.6 The following is a picture of the great Indigo Uprising which witnessed strong unity among peasants across religious lines.

Which one of the following best explains the significance of this unity during the Indigo Revolt?

(a) It transformed the revolt into a violent armed struggle.
(b) It revealed the secular nature of peasant resistance against colonial exploitation.
(c) It led to immediate abolition of British rule in Bengal.
(d) It resulted in the formation of a political party.

Ans. (b) It revealed the secular nature of peasant resistance against colonial exploitation.

Q.7 Identify the key difference between the Deccan Riots (1875) and the Munda Uprising (1899.1900).

(a) The Deccan Riots were led by tribal leaders, while the Munda Uprising was led by peasants.

(b) The Deccan Riots focused on exploitation by moneylenders, while the Munda Uprising focused on land rights and exploitation by landlords and colonial officials.

(c) The Munda Uprising resulted in the passing of the Deccan Land Act, while the Deccan Riots resulted in the reintroduction of Khunt-Katti system.

(d) Both movements were non-violent protests against British policies.

Ans. (b) The Deccan Riots focused on exploitation by moneylenders, while the Munda Uprising focused on land rights and exploitation by landlords and colonial officials.

Q.8 Identify the tribal leader whose resistance against British colonial policies in Chota Nagpur combined defense of land rights and opposition to exploitation by landlords and moneylenders.

(a) John Baptist led missionary conversions among tribals.

(b) Tomma Dora led a rebellion in Eastern Godavari.

(c) Birsa Munda mobilised the Munda community and resisted colonial authority.

(d) Harish Chandra Mukerjee opposed Sati practice in Bengal.

Ans. (c) Birsa Munda mobilised the Munda community and resisted colonial authority.

Assertion-Reason Questions

Given below are two statements marked as Assertion (A) and Reason (R). Read the two statements and choose the corrects answer from the codes given below.

(a) Both A and R are true and R is the correct explanation for A.

(b) Both A and R are true, but R is not the correct explanation for A.

(c) A is false, but R is true.

(d) A is true, but R is false.

Q.1 Assertion (A) The Indigo Revolt of 1859 forced peasants to grow indigo against their will.

Reason (R) Indigo planters paid peasants advances and then compelled them to sell indigo at very low prices.

Ans. (a) Both A and R are true and R is the correct explanation of A.

Q.2 Assertion (A) The Indigo Revolt was secular in character, uniting both Hindu and Muslim peasants.

Reason (R) Educated Indians like Harish Chandra Mukerjee and Dinabandhu Mitra supported peasants through articles and plays.

Ans. (b) Both A and R are true, but R is not the correct explanation for A.

Q.3 Assertion (A) The Deccan Riots led to the arrest of rebel leaders, breaking the morale of peasants.

Reason (R) The Ramosi tribal revolt in Bombay province was successful due to strong tribal unity.

Ans. (c) A is false, but R is true.

Q.4 Assertion (A) The Deccan Riots (1875) were caused by peasant indebtedness and exploitation by moneylenders.

Reason (R) The British government passed the Deccan Land Act to protect peasants from borrowing money.

Ans. (d) A is true, but R is false.

Q.5 Assertion (A) Birsa Munda's leadership in the Munda Uprising aimed to restore traditional tribal land rights.

Reason (R) The British land revenue policies had destroyed the Khunt-Katti system, causing exploitation by landlords and moneylenders.

Ans. (a) Both A and R are true and R is the correct explanation for A.

Very Short Answer Type Questions

Q.1 The image given below shows the cover page of the play Nil Darpan. *Source: banerjees peaks*

Name the author who wrote the play Nil Darpan, in which he portrayed the suffering of peasants.

Ans. Dinabandhu Mitra

Q.2 .... translated Nil Darpan into English.

Ans. Michael Madhusudan Dutta

Q.3 **During the Indigo Revolt of 1859, peasants in Bengal and Bihar were forced to grow indigo instead of food crops. Many faced torture and attacks on their homes when they resisted. Educated Indians like Harish Chandra Mukerjee and Dinabandhu Mitra supported the peasants.**

What was the significance of this movement in colonial India?

Ans. It was one of the earliest mass civil disobedience movements in India and forced the colonial government to protect peasants from being forced to grow indigo.

Q.4 **During the Deccan Riots of 1875, peasants in Poona and Ahmadnagar attacked the houses of moneylenders, burnt debt records, and destroyed property.** ***(Source: the deccan)***

State any one impact this movement had on British colonial policies.

Ans. The British government passed the Deccan Land Act (1879), which restricted loans on mortgaged property and made the registration of contracts and mortgages compulsory, to protect peasants from exploitation by moneylenders.

Q.5 **.............. led the Deccan Riots in Poona and Ahmadnagar.**

Ans. Kenglia

Q.6 **The traditional land system of the Mundas was called ....**

Ans. Khunt-Katti

Q.7 **During the Munda Uprising (1899-1900), Birsa Munda led the tribal community of Chhota Nagpur to resist British exploitation, attack government offices, and reclaim traditional land rights. Mention any one impact of this movement on British colonial policies.**

Ans. The British reintroduced the Khunt Katti system to restore tribal land rights and reduce exploitation.

TYPE - 2 4 Marks

Short Answer Type Questions

Q.1 **How did the Indigo Uprising influence the colonial government's policies towards peasants? Explain.**

Ans. The Indigo Uprising (1859) forced the British government to introduce corrective measures which are given below

- Governor Grant issued a proclamation declaring that peasants could not be forced to grow indigo against their will.
- The government appointed the Indigo Commission to investigate complaints of peasants and planters.
- These steps limited the arbitrary power of European planters over the peasants.
- Indigo plantations gradually shifted from Bengal to Bihar and Uttar Pradesh due to reduced planter control.

Q.2 **With reference to the below news extract given, state any four methods that were used by indigo planters and which led to widespread resentment among peasants in Bengal and Bihar?**

Indigo Revolt in Bengal

They say that the color of revolution is red. Not always. Sometimes, it's blue. It was the summer of 1859 in Bengal when thousands of ryots (peasants) refused to grow indigo for the European planters (owners of land and indigo factories). It was a show of rage and undying resolve. It became one of the most remarkable peasant movements of Indian history. It came to be called the ***Neel Bidroha*** or the **Indigo Revolt**.

Indigo was being cultivated in Bengal since the end of the **18th century**. It was practiced mainly in two forms, the **Nij-abad** and the **Ryoti**. In the Nij or "own" system, the planter produced indigo on lands that he directly controlled. In the Ryoti cultivation, the ryots cultivated indigo on their own lands as part of a contract with the planters.

A painting of an indigo factory

The planters gained land rights in a number of ways. They took waste or unoccupied lands on temporary or permanent leases from the Zamindars. They also acquired Zamindari and Taluqdari rights. At times, Indigo cultivation would also be carried out on the lands of ryots who had died without an heir or who had abandoned their villages.

Ans. The methods adopted by indigo planters created deep resentment among peasants are as follows

(i) Peasants were forced to cultivate Indigo instead of food crops, which caused hunger and poverty in their families.

(ii) Planters cheated peasants by unfair measurement of the land and made them sign oppressive contracts.

(iii) Advances were given to peasants, but Indigo was purchased at very low prices, increasing their indebtedness.

(iv) Those who resisted faced torture, confinement, and attacks on their homes, leading to anger and rebellion.

Q.3 **In 1875, peasants in the Deccan region rose in revolt against moneylenders. They attacked the houses of mahajans, burnt debt records, and destroyed property in districts like Poona and Ahmadnagar.**

Based on the above report, state any four reasons for the Deccan Riots of 1875.

Ans. The reasons of Deccan riots are as follows

- The Deccan economy was mainly dependent on cotton cultivation, making peasants vulnerable to market fluctuations.
- A sudden fall in international cotton prices in 1870 left peasants unable to repay their loans.
- Moneylenders charged very high rates of interest and exploited peasants through debt.
- Moneylenders seized peasant lands and property, transferring ownership to themselves, which created widespread anger.

Q.4 Discuss any four achievements of Birsa Munda that justify his recognition as a heroic tribal leader in Indian history.

Ans. The achievements of Birsa Munda that justify his recognition as a heroic tribal leader in Indian history are as follows

- Birsa Munda united the Munda tribes of Chota Nagpur and led a strong resistance against British colonial authority.
- He fought to restore the traditional Khunt-Katti system, protecting collective tribal ownership of land.
- He mobilised tribals against exploitation by landlords, moneylenders and forced labour practices.
- His movement became a lasting symbol of tribal resistance and compelled the British to reintroduce the Khunt-Katti system.

TYPE - 3 — 8 Marks

Long Answer Type Questions

Q.1 European indigo planters in Bengal and Bihar forced peasants to grow indigo instead of food crops. Peasants were cheated through unfair contracts and paid very low prices. Some leaders organised a boycott of indigo cultivation and peasants revolted. Alarmed by the situation, the colonial government appointed a commission to inquire into peasant grievances.

(a) Mention the name of the commission appointed by the British government after the Indigo Revolt. Explain the indigo protest movement.

(b) Explain any four effects of the Indigo Revolt on colonial policies and Indian society.

Ans. (a) The British government appointed the Indigo Commission to inquire into the grievances of the peasants. The Indigo protest movement can be explained as follows

- The peasants organised a collective boycott of indigo cultivation and refused to sow indigo despite threats, torture, and false court cases by European planters.
- Leaders like Digambar Biswas and Vishnu Charan Biswas mobilised peasants, while educated Indians like Harish Chandra Mukerjee and Dinabandhu Mitra supported the movement through newspapers and literary works like Nil Darpan.
- The movement remained largely non-violent and united, with Hindu and Muslim peasants participating together, which forced the colonial government to intervene and review its indigo policy.

(b) The effects of the Indigo Revolt on colonial policies and Indian society.

- The colonial government declared that no peasant could be forced to grow Indigo against his will.
- The findings of the commission reduced the arbitrary power of European planters.
- Indigo cultivation declined in Bengal and shifted to Bihar and Uttar Pradesh.
- The revolt demonstrated the power of organised and largely non-violent mass protest and encouraged future movements.

Q.2 Peasants in the Deccan region first tried to socially boycott moneylenders. When this failed, they rose in revolt in the Poona and Ahmadnagar districts. They attacked the houses of moneylenders, burnt debt records, and destroyed property.

With reference to the Deccan Riots, answer the following questions.

(a) Describe any four features of the protest during the Deccan Riots.

(b) Explain any four impacts of the Deccan Riots on British colonial policy.

Ans. (a) The features of the protest during the Deccan Riots are

- The peasants initially tried to protest peacefully by socially boycotting moneylenders.
- When the boycott failed, peasants revolted violently in the Poona and Ahmadnagar districts.

- They attacked the houses of moneylenders, burnt debt records and destroyed property to free themselves from debt.
- The revolt was led by Kenglia, but his arrest reduced the morale and strength of the rebels.

(b) The impacts of the Deccan Riots on British colonial policy are

- The British government passed the Deccan Land Act of 1879 to protect peasants from exploitation.
- The Act restricted moneylenders from giving loans on the mortgage of peasant land.
- It made the registration of loan contracts and mortgages compulsory in government offices.
- The British government realised that peasants were suffereing due to heavy debt, high revenue demand and exploitation.

Q.3 **Discuss the circumstances, nature of the protest, and impact of the Munda Uprising under Birsa Munda.**

Ans. The circumstances, nature of the protest and impact of the Munda Uprising under Birsa Munda are as follows

Circumstances of the Munda Uprising Chota Nagpur

- The Mundas lived in the Chota Nagpur region and followed the Khunt-Katti system of collective land ownership.
- British land revenue policies destroyed this system, imposed heavy taxes, and encouraged exploitation by zamindars and moneylenders.
- The Mundas lost their customary rights over forests and were forced to provide unpaid labour.
- Disappointment with missionaries, who tried to convert them to Christianity, increased their anger against colonial authorities.

Nature of the Protest

- Birsa Munda emerged as the leader and declared that land belonged to the Mundas, calling for complete freedom from British control.
- The Mundas attacked police stations, churches, and government offices with traditional weapons and offered determined resistance to colonial rule.

Impact of the Uprising

- The British government was compelled to reintroduce the Khunt-Katti system to pacify the Munda community.
- Laws were enacted to restrict the transfer of tribal land to non-tribals (dikus), and provided some protection against exploitation by moneylenders, landlords and traders.

4

GROWTH OF NATIONALISM

Swadeshi Movement

- The early 20th century was an important period in the growth of Indian nationalism.
- The Partition of Bengal in 1905 created widespread dissatisfaction among the Indian people.
- This led to the Anti-Partition Movement, including the Swadeshi and Boycott Movements, which encouraged the use of Indian goods and rejection of foreign goods.
- These movements increased political awareness and united people in the struggle against British rule.
- During the same period, the Muslim League was founded to protect the political interests of the Muslim community.

Swadeshi Movement

Partition of Bengal (1905)

- The partition of Bengal was announced by Lord Curzon on 20th July, 1905 and was implemented on 16th October, 1905.
- Bengal was divided into two parts
- **Western Bengal** This included proper Bengal (Western districts), Bihar and Orissa, with Calcutta as its capital and a total population of approximately 54 million.
- **Eastern Bengal and Assam** This included Dacca, Rajshahi, Chittagong, Assam and Malda, with Dacca as its capital and a total population of approximately 31 million.
- The official reason given for the partition was that Bengal was too large to be administered efficiently.
- The real motive was to weaken Bengali nationalism, reduce the importance of Calcutta as the main centre of Anti-British politics, and divide Hindus and Muslims to break their unity.

Lord Curzon

Anti-Partition Movement: Swadeshi and Boycott Movement

- The anti-partition agitation soon developed into the Swadeshi and Boycott Movement, which had several phases

First Phase: Initial Reaction

- The partition was implemented on 16th October, 1905, which was observed as a day of mourning and protest throughout Bengal.
- People observed hartals, bathed in the Ganga and sang Rabindranath Tagore's patriotic song *Banglar Mati, Banglar Jal.*
- Hindus and Muslims exchanged and tied Raksha Bandhan threads to symbolise unity and brotherhood.
- Mass meetings were held, petitions and memorials were submitted to the government, and prominent leaders such as Surendranath Banerjee and Ananda Mohan Bose led the agitation.
- The English press in India, which included the Statesman and the Pioneer, initially criticised the partition.

Second Phase : Self and Help (Atma Sakti)

Rabindranath Tagore

- Rabindranath Tagore and Aswini Kumar Dutta appealed to the people of Bengal to start Atma Sakti.
- Rabindranath Tagore urged the people to take up constructive work through his article Swadeshi Samaj.
- The Dawn Society, which was founded by Satis Chandra Mukherjee, promoted national education.
- Indigenous institutions such as Braja Mohan College at Barisal and the Bengal Technical Institute (later Jadavpur University) were established.
- Leaders like P.C. Ray encouraged Swadeshi industries, banks and insurance companies.

Third Phase: Boycott of British Goods

Bipin Chandra Pal

Krishna Kumar Mitra

- The idea of boycott was first suggested by Krishna Kumar Mitra in his journal Sanjivani (July 1905).
- The proposal was formally accepted at a Calcutta Town Hall meeting on 7th August, 1905.
- Newspapers such as Bande Mataram, Sandhya and Yugantar strongly supported the boycott.
- Bipin Chandra Pal strongly criticised the petition and prayer policy of the Moderates in his journal New India.
- In his pamphlet New Lamps for the Old, Aurobindo Ghosh appealed to the people to unite and support the movement against British rule.

Fourth Phase: Spread of Swadeshi

- In the fourth phase, the leadership of the movement passed into the hands of student volunteers, who became the most active participants.
- Students organised picketing in front of shops that sold British goods and persuaded people to buy indigenous products instead.
- They shouted slogans like *Bande Mataram* and came out of schools and colleges to join the agitation.
- A large number of volunteer organisations were formed in Calcutta and Eastern Bengal to spread the message of boycott and Swadeshi. Some of the important organisations included the Brati Sangha, Swadeshbandhav Samiti, Anushilan Samiti, Sadhana and Suhrid Samiti.
- In the districts, the Saha community was targeted because they refused to accept the boycott of foreign goods, which led to social tensions.
- The government adopted repressive measures against schools and colleges whose students participated in the movement.
- Students were fined, expelled and beaten with lathis by the police, while government grants to institutions were withdrawn if their students joined the agitation.
- Despite repression, the student volunteers played a crucial role in spreading the boycott and Swadeshi message to the masses and kept the spirit of nationalism alive.

Fifth Phase: Revolutionary Phase

- Brutal repression by the British pushed many youths towards revolutionary nationalism.
- Secret societies such as the Anushilan Samiti and the Maniktala group planned assassinations of British officials.
- The discovery of the Maniktala Bomb Factory in 1908 revealed the extent of revolutionary activities.

Causes of the Movement

- The partition of Bengal was seen as a deliberate insult to Bengali pride and unity.
- Lord Curzon's repressive policies, such as the Municipality Act of 1899 and the Universities Act of 1904 had already angered the people.

EXAM ORIENTED QUESTIONS

TYPE - 1 　　1 Mark

Multiple Choice Questions

Q.1 While announcing the division of Bengal in 1905, the British government put forward an administrative justification for this decision.

Identify the official reason given by the British for the Partition of Bengal.

(a) To reduce communal tensions.
(b) To punish nationalist leaders.
(c) To make Bengal easier to administer due to its vast size.
(d) To create a Muslim majority province.

Ans. (c) To make Bengal easier to administer due to its vast size.

Q.2 Identify the contribution of Rabindranath Tagore during the Swadeshi Movement.

(a) He led violent protests against British officials.
(b) He promoted constructive work and national education through Atma Sakti.
(c) He organised the boycott of British goods and Swadeshi industries.
(d) He formed secret revolutionary societies to fight British rule.

Ans. (b) He promoted constructive work and national education through Atma Sakti.

Q.3 Which of the following best describes the public response to the Partition of Bengal in 1905?

(a) Violent attacks on British officials
(b) Hartals, patriotic songs, symbolic unity, meetings and petitions
(c) Only boycotting British goods
(d) No protests

Ans. (b) Hartals, patriotic songs, symbolic unity, meetings and petitions

Q.4 Who among the following leaders guided the people of Bengal during the anti-partition protests of 1905?

(a) Bal Gangadhar Tilak
(b) Surendranath Banerjee and Ananda Mohan Bose
(c) Lala Lajpat Rai
(d) Bipin Chandra Pal

Ans. (b) Surendranath Banerjee and Ananda Mohan Bose

Q.5 Who among the following leaders first suggested the idea of boycotting British goods during the Anti-Partition Movement?

(a) Bipin Chandra Pal　　(b) Aurobindo Ghosh
(c) Krishna Kumar Mitra　　(d) Surendranath Banerjee

Ans. (c) Krishna Kumar Mitra

Q.6 The following is an image depicting the Swadeshi and Boycott Movement, highlighting the role of students and volunteer organisations in spreading the message of nationalism.

Which one of the following best explains the contribution of students during this phase?

(a) They focused mainly on petitions to the government to demand reforms.
(b) They organised picketing, promoted indigenous products and spread nationalist ideas,
(c) They avoided participation in public agitation and confined themselves to academic activities.
(d) They led violent attacks on British officials and property.

Ans. (b) They organised picketing, promoted indigenous products and spread nationalist ideas.

Q.7 Which of the following phases of the Swadeshi and Boycott Movement best reflects the principle of promoting self-reliance in education, industry and culture, similar to modern initiatives that encourage domestic development and innovation?

(a) First Phase-Initial Reaction, when people observed hartals, sang patriotic songs and tied Rakhis as a symbol of unity.
(b) Second Phase-Self- Help (Atma Sakti), when leaders encouraged Swadeshi industries, banking, educational institutions and constructive work.

(c) Third Phase - Boycott of British Goods, when leaders promoted petitions and pamphlets against British rule.
(d) Fifth Phase - Revolutionary Phase, when secret societies planned assassinations of British officials.

Ans. (b) Second Phase–Self-Help (Atma Sakti), when leaders encouraged Swadeshi industries, banks, education and constructive work.

Q.8 Which of the following developments is considered the most significant achievement of the Swadeshi Movement in strengthening Indian nationalism?
(a) The spread of revolutionary terrorism in Bengal.
(b) The promotion of Swadeshi industries and national education.
(c) The support extended by the British press.
(d) The withdrawal of government grants to schools.

Ans. (b) The promotion of Swadeshi industries and national education.

Q.9 The extract given below refers to a contemporary report on the Swadeshi and Boycott Movement during the Anti-Partition agitation in Bengal (1905 - 1908). Which of the following factors contributed to the decline of the Swadeshi Movement by 1908?

THE BENGAL TIMES
Special Report
SWADESHI MOVEMENT FACES DECLINE
LEADERS ARRESTED, MOVEMENT WEAKENS

Calcutta, 1908 —
The Swadeshi Movement, once a powerful force in Bengal, is now in decline. Key nationalist leaders including Tilak and Lajpat Rai have been arrested or exiled. The British authorities have intensified repression, closing schools, withdrawing grants, and conducting harsh crackdowns on protesters.

P : Severe repression by the British government, including arrests and lathi charges
Q : Imprisonment, exile, and withdrawal of key nationalist leaders
R : Immediate acceptance of Indian demands by the British authorities
S : Strong and sustained participation of peasants and workers

(a) P and Q (b) Q and R (c) P and S (d) R and S

Ans. (a) P and Q

Q.10 Identify the key reason for the foundation of the All-India Muslim League in 1906.
(a) To overthrow the British government and join the Indian National Congress.
(b) To create a separate political platform to protect Muslim interests and ensure representation.
(c) To promote Urdu as the sole official language across India.
(d) To merge with Hindu leaders and form a joint nationalist organisation.

Ans. (b) To create a separate political platform to protect Muslim interests and ensure representation.

Assertion - Reason Questions

Given below are two statements marked as Assertion (A) and Reason (R). Read the two statements and choose the corrects answer from the codes given below.

Codes
(a) Both A and R are true and R is the correct explanation for A.
(b) Both A and R are true, but R is not the correct explanation for A.
(c) A is false, but R is true.
(d) A is true, but R is false.

Q.1 **Assertion** (A) The Swadeshi and Boycott Movement encouraged Indians to use indigenous goods and reject British products.

Reason (R) The movement was launched as a response to the Partition of Bengal in 1905, which aimed to divide Hindu and Muslim communities.

Ans. (a) Both A and R are true and R is the correct explanation for A.

Q.2 **Assertion** (A) The Swadeshi Movement immediately achieved complete independence for India.

Reason (R) The movement spread because the British government fully supported the use of indigenous goods and national education.

Ans. (d) A is true, but R is false.

Q.3 **Assertion** (A) The Surat Split of 1907 weakened the unity of the Indian National Congress.

Reason (R) The Swadeshi Movement faced severe repression from the British, including arrests, fines, and bans on patriotic slogans.

Ans. (b) Both A and R are true, but R is not the correct explanation for A.

Q.4 **Assertion** (A) The boycott of British goods during the Swadeshi Movement was largely confined to the middle class.

Reason (R) British goods were cheaper than Swadeshi products, making it difficult for peasants and workers to participate.

Ans. (a) Both A and R are true and R is the correct explanation for A.

(iii) He supported the establishment of educational institutions such as the Bengal Technical Institute and the Dawn Society to promote national education.

(iv) Through his writings, articles, and speeches, he spread nationalist ideas and inspired people to adopt self-reliance and pride in Indian culture.

Q.4 The British implemented the Partition of Bengal in 1905, dividing the province into Western Bengal and Eastern Bengal and Assam. In response, mass protests, hartals, petitions, and the Swadeshi and Boycott Movements emerged.

In the above context, analyse the impact of the Swadeshi and Boycott Movements on the Indian Nationalist Movement.

Ans. The Swadeshi and Boycott Movements had significant impacts on the growth of Indian nationalism

- They united people across communities and regions, fostering a sense of national consciousness and collective identity against British rule.
- The movements promoted economic self-reliance by encouraging the use of indigenous goods, and the growth of Swadeshi industries, banks, and insurance companies.
- They inspired educational and cultural development through initiatives like the Dawn Society, National College, and Bengal Technical Institute, promoting national education.
- The movements instilled a new militant spirit in Indian nationalism, paving the way for later mass movements such as the Non-Cooperation and Civil Disobedience Movements.

Q.5 The Swadeshi Movement inspired nationalism but faced many challenges.

With reference to the Anti-Partition Movement, answer the following questions.

State any four limitations of the Swadeshi Movement.

Ans. Four limitations of the Swadeshi Movement were as follows

(i) The movement faced ruthless repression, including lathi charges, arrests and bans on patriotic slogans like *Bande Mataram*.

(ii) The Surat Split of 1907 weakened the unity of the Indian National Congress.

(iii) Tilak was jailed, Lajpat Rai exiled and Aurobindo retired from politics.

(iv) Peasants and workers were not effectively mobilised, and the Muslim masses largely remained distant.

Q.6 In 1906, the All-India Muslim League was formed to safeguard the political interests of Muslims in India.

Source: Historical records

Based on the above report, state any four circumstances that led to the formation of the All-India Muslim League.

Ans. The formation of the All - India Muslim League in 1906 was influenced by several important circumstances

(i) Many Muslims felt politically alienated from the Indian National Congress, fearing that it was dominated by Hindu leaders and would not protect Muslim interests.

(ii) The Urdu-Hindi controversy created a sense of separate cultural and political identity among Muslims, increasing the desire for a distinct political platform.

(iii) The Partition of Bengal in 1905 was welcomed by Muslims in East Bengal, as it offered them better opportunities in education, employment and administration.

(iv) The British authorities encouraged Muslim leaders to organise separately to counterbalance the growing influence of the Congress and maintain communal loyalty.

TYPE - 3 — 8 Marks

Long Answer Type Questions

Q.1 Bengal has been divided into two parts; this is a blow to the unity of the nation□

Source: Contemporary reports, 1905

With reference to the Partition of Bengal, answer the following questions.

(a) State any four causes for the Partition of Bengal.

(b) Discuss any two reasons each for why many Indians saw the Partition as a political move rather than an administrative necessity.

Ans. (a) Four causes for the Partition of Bengal are as follows

(i) The British claimed that Bengal was too vast to be administered efficiently, giving this as the official reason.

(ii) The growth of Bengali nationalism and anti-British activities made the province politically sensitive.

(iii) The British wanted to divide Hindus and Muslims geographically to weaken their unity.

(iv) Previous repressive measures by Lord Curzon, such as the Municipality Act (1899) and Universities Act (1904), had already alienated educated Indians.

(b) Many Indians saw the partition as a political move rather than an administrative necessity because

- The division weakened the influence of Calcutta as the centre of anti-British politics.
- It aimed to curb Bengali nationalism and consolidate British control over the province.

The administrative justification was doubted because

- The timing and manner of the decision, without adequate consultation with Indian leaders, raised suspicion.
- The official claim of administrative efficiency did not convince Indians, as other large provinces had not been divided similarly.

Q.2 Discuss any eight effects of British repressive measures on nationalist activities between 1905 and 1908.

Ans. Effects of British repressive measures on nationalist activities between 1905 and 1908 are as follows

(i) Disruption of Organisational Activities Repression, fines, and police action hampered meetings and local organisation.

(ii) Punishment of Students Student activists faced expulsions, lathi charges and other forms of physical punishment.

(iii) Withdrawal of Grants Institutions whose students joined protests lost government funding.

(iv) Legal Restrictions Laws and regulations limited the freedom of nationalist activities.

(v) Weakening of Moderate Leadership Key leaders were jailed, exiled or forced to retire, reducing the influence of the moderates.

(vi) Radicalisation of Youth Harsh measures pushed many young people toward revolutionary and militant methods.

(vii) Rise of Boycott and Swadeshi Frustration with ineffective petitions encouraged economic resistance and self-reliance.

(viii) Emergence of Revolutionary Societies Events like the discovery of the Maniktala Bomb Factory in 1908 exemplified the turn to secret and violent activism.

Q.3 In 1906, an organisation was formed by prominent Muslim Leaders to protect Muslim political interests in India.

Source: Historical records

(a) Identify the organisation that was formed and State any three objectives of the organisation.

(b) Discuss any four impacts of the organisation on Indian politics in the early 20th century.

Ans. (a) The organisation formed was the All-India Muslim League.

Three objectives of the League were as follows

(i) To promote loyalty to the British government and to assure the government that Muslims would support British authority in India.

(ii) To protect and advance the political rights and interests of Muslims in India.

(iii) To prevent hostility between Muslims and other communities, while safeguarding Muslim interests.

(b) Four impacts of the formation of Muslim League on the Indian politics were as follows

(i) It provided Muslims with a separate political platform to represent and protect their rights and interests.

(ii) It increased political organisation among Muslims, allowing them to participate effectively in legislative councils and public debates.

(iii) It contributed to a communal political consciousness, that influencing the dynamics between Hindu and Muslim communities in India.

(iv) It shaped the future political landscape of India, ultimately playing a key role in the demand for Pakistan and the partition of India in 1947.

5

GANDHIAN NATIONALISM (1916-1922)

- The period from 1916 to 1922 marked the emergence of Mahatma Gandhi as the most influential leader of the Indian National Movement.
- Gandhiji introduced new methods of struggle such as Satyagraha, non-violence and mass participation during this phase.
- The repressive policies of the British government after the First World War, especially the Rowlatt Act, intensified Indian resentment (anger).
- Gandhian nationalism aimed to unite Indians across regions, classes and religions in a common fight against colonial rule.
- Movements like the Anti-Rowlatt agitation, the Khilafat Movement, and the Non-Cooperation Movement transformed the freedom struggle into a nationwide mass movement.

Mahatma Gandhi Addressing at a Public Meeting

The Rowlatt Act

- In 1917, the British appointed a committee under Justice Sydney Rowlatt to investigate the revolutionary crimes.
- In March 1919, the Rowlatt Act was passed by the British Government.

Reasons behind the Rowlatt Act

- **Fear of Revolutionary Activities** The British government feared the growth of revolutionary and terrorist activities in India after the First World War.
- **Influence of the Russian Revolution** The success of the Russian Revolution in 1917 alarmed the British and they feared that similar uprisings could take place in India.
- **Post-War Economic and Social Unrest** Economic hardships such as inflation, unemployment and food shortages after the war had caused widespread dissatisfaction and protests among Indians.
- **Recommendations of the Rowlatt Committee** The Rowlatt Committee recommended strict laws to suppress revolutionary nationalism, which directly led to the enactment of the Rowlatt Act.
- **Extension of Emergency Powers** The British wanted to continue the wartime emergency powers provided under the Defence of India Act of 1915, even after the war ended.
- **Control Over Nationalist Leaders** The British wanted the authority to arrest and detain nationalist leaders without trial, which helped them to maintain control over political opposition.
- **Distrust of Indian Loyalty** Despite the support provided by Indians during the First World War, the British doubted the loyalty of Indians, which prompted them to impose repressive measures.

Main Terms of Rowlatt Act

- The Act empowered the government to arrest and detain any individual on the basis of suspicion, without trial (for upto 2 years).
- It allowed imprisonment without producing the accused before a court of law.
- The Act permitted trials to be held without jury.
- The accused was denied the right to know the evidence against him.
- There was no provision for appeal against the judgement passed under this act.
- The government was given wide powers to suppress freedom of speech, press and movement.
- The act extended the extraordinary powers of the Defence of India Act even after the First World War had ended.

Agitation (Satyagraha) against the Rowlatt Act

- Mahatma Gandhi strongly criticised the Act and described it as a law of 'No appeal, no vakil, no law,' as it denied civil liberties.
- Muhammad Ali Jinnah strongly opposed the Rowlatt Act and warned of its dangerous consequences.
- In 1915, Mahatma Gandhi had established the Satyagraha Ashram at Ahmedabad to train the people about the principles of non-violent resistance.
- In February 1919, he formed the Satyagraha Sabha in Bombay to organise opposition to the Rowlatt Act.
- He called for a nationwide hartal on 30th March 1919, which was later postponed to 6th April, 1919.
- Hartals, processions and demonstrations were held across India, which showed widespread public participation.
- Police fired on demonstrators in Delhi on 30th March, which witnessed the death of ten people.
- Gandhiji intensified the movement by urging satyagrahis to disobey laws which were related to banned literature and newspaper registration.
- Four books, including 'Hind Swaraj' had been banned, but volunteers were openly selling them as an act of defiance (disobey).
- Gandhiji was arrested and sent back to Bombay when he tried to travel to Delhi and Punjab to control the movement.
- Violence broke out in Ahmedabad, which led the government to impose martial law.
- Moderate leaders such as Surendranath Banerjee, Tej Bahadur Sapru, Srinivas Sastri and Annie Besant opposed Gandhiji's method of Satyagraha.
- Meanwhile Younger nationalist leaders and radical elements of the Home Rule League supported Gandhiji's move.

Jallianwala Bagh Massacre (13th April, 1919)

Jallianwala Bagh Massacre

- In Amritsar, Punjab, nationalist leaders Dr. Saifuddin Kitchlew and Dr. Satyapal were arrested on 10th April, 1919 under the Rowlatt Act.
- To protest against their arrest and the repressive policies of the government, thousands of people gathered peacefully at Jallianwala Bagh on 13th April, 1919.
- The gathering included men, women and children who had assembled on the occasion of Baisakhi.
- Brigadier-General Reginald Dyer entered the enclosed ground with troops and ordered them to open fire on the unarmed crowd without giving any warning.
- The only exit of the park was blocked, leaving the crowd trapped without an exit.
- According to official British figures, 379 people were killed, though Indian estimates placed the number of deaths much higher.
- That same day, martial law was imposed throughout Punjab to suppress public protest.
- A series of humiliating and inhuman punishments were imposed on the people to terrorise them.
- People were publicly beaten and villagers were forced to crawl (move on hands and knees) on the ground in streets.
- Prisoners were kept in open cages and overcrowded trucks for long hours under harsh conditions.
- News of these unhumane atrocities spread rapidly across India and ignited a wave of anger, fear and hatred against British rule.
- Rabindranath Tagore renounced his title of Knighthood in protest and wrote a powerful letter to Lord Chelmsford condemning British injustice.

Rabindranath Tagore

Outcome of the Agitation

- The agitation against the Rowlatt Act failed largely due to a lack of proper organisation and central coordinating authority.
- The Satyagraha Sabha remained mainly engaged in propaganda work, while the Indian National Congress refrained from providing direct leadership in the movement.
- The movement was more effective in urban areas than in rural ones, where participation was often driven by local issues such as price rise and scarcity of essential goods.
- Historian Judith Brown observed that Bombay and Gujarat were the core areas of the movement, while response in other regions remained weak.
- Historian Bipan Chandra pointed out that protests were frequently accompanied by violence, particularly in Punjab, which had already suffered wartime repression and forced recruitment.
- Due to the spread of violence, Gandhiji decided to call off the movement.
- The most significant outcome of the agitation was the emergence of Gandhiji as an all-India leader for the first time.
- The Rowlatt Act and the Jallianwala Bagh massacre shattered Gandhiji's faith in British justice, consequently he described the colonial government as a 'Satanic Government'.

Passive Resistance: Khilafat and Non-Cooperation Movement (1919-1922)

- The period from 1919 to 1922 witnessed the growth of satyagraha and passive resistance under the leadership of Mahatma Gandhi.
- During this phase, the Khilafat and Non-Cooperation Movements were launched to oppose British rule through peaceful and non-violent satyagraha.

Launch of the Khilafat Movement

- After the First World War, the Allied Powers defeated Turkey and depopsed the Turkish Sultan from the political power who was also known as the Khalifa.
- The Khalifa was regarded as the spiritual head of the Muslim world, and his humiliation deeply hurt the religious sentiments of Indian Muslims.
- Indian Muslims demanded that the Khalifa should retain control over Muslim holy places and should be left with sufficient territory after the war.
- To organise the movement, leaders such as Shaukat Ali and Mohammad Ali formed the All-India Khilafat Committee in Bombay, in 1919.
- At the All-India Khilafat Conference held in Delhi in November 1919, the leaders decided to adopt the method of Non-Cooperation with the British government.
- In April 1920, Shaukat Ali publicly warned that if Muslim demands were not met the Hindus and Muslims would jointly launch a Movement of Non-Cooperation.
- Mahatma Gandhi supported the Khilafat Movement, in order to promote Hindu-Muslim unity and became the President of the All-India Khilafat Committee.
- The Khilafat issue provided Gandhiji with an opportunity to link religious sentiments with the wider political struggle against British rule in India.
- The Central Khilafat Committee meeting at Allahabad formally adopted the programme of Non-Cooperation in June 1920.

Shaukat Ali and Mohammad Ali

REVISION NOTES

Causes of the Non-Cooperation Movement

- **Disappointment after World War I** Indians gave huge support to Britain during the war with money, soldiers, and loyalty and expected self-Government in return. But the Montagu-Chelmsford Reforms (1919) fell short of granting real autonomy, which caused deep frustration.
- **Economic Hardship** The war caused a hike in prices and inflation. Peasants had to pay extra rent and taxes. Scarcity of cloth, salt and kerosene worsened misery.
- **Impact of International Movements** The Bolshevik Revolution (1917) in Russia demonstrated that even the most powerful autocracies could be brought down. Movements in Ireland and Egypt against British rule inspired Indian leaders to believe freedom was possible.
- **Rowlatt Act (1919)** The Act allowed imprisonment without trial for two years and denial of legal rights. It was seen as a betrayal of promises of reform and provoked strong resentment.
- **Jallianwala Bagh Massacre (1919)** General Dyer's brutal firing on a peaceful crowd at Amritsar shocked the nation. Martial law and humiliating punishments in Punjab deepened anger.
- **Khilafat Issue** The deposition of the Turkish Sultan (Khalifa) after World War I offended Muslim sentiments.
- **Youth Aspiration for Swaraj** Indian youth were inspired by the idea of self-rule (Swaraj) and were ready to sacrifice for it. Their enthusiasm gave momentum to the movement.

C.R. Das

Annie Besant

Launching the Non-Cooperation Movement

- Mahatma Gandhi introduced resolution on Non-Cooperation before the Indian National Congress at its Calcutta Session in September 1920. Although leaders such as C. R. Das, Annie Besant, and Madan Mohan Malaviya initially opposed the resolution but it was eventually passed.
- The programme of Non-Cooperation was finally endorsed at the Nagpur Session of the Congress in December 1920. This Session also reorganised the Congress to make it a truly national and mass-based organisation.
- A Working Committee consisting of 15 members was formed to lead the movement.
- An All-India Committee of 350 members was created and Congress committees were established in towns, districts and villages.
- The membership fee was reduced to four annas (25 paise) to encourage participation by peasants and the rural poor.
- The programme of Non-Cooperation included the surrender of titles and honours, boycott of government schools, law courts, councils, and foreign goods.
- It also emphasised the promotion of Khadi and the Charkha, the establishment of national schools and the setting up of arbitration courts to settle disputes.

Course of the Movement

- Between January and March 1921, large numbers of students boycotted government schools and colleges and many lawyers suspended their legal practice.
- Prominent leaders such as C. R. Das, Motilal Nehru, Rajendra Prasad and Sardar Vallabhbhai Patel withdrew from the courts to support the movement.
- The boycott of foreign goods intensified, and people actively promoted the use of Khadi and spinning of yarn from July to November 1921.
- The visit of the Prince of Wales in November 1921 was boycotted across India, and widespread hartals and demonstrations were organised.

People Participated in the Non-Cooperation Movement

- During this phase, jail-bharo campaigns were launched and thousands of volunteers courted arrest.
- In early 1922, Mahatma Gandhi planned to begin a no-tax campaign in Bardoli, in Gujarat as part of a wider programme of mass civil disobedience.

Suspension of the Movement

- On 5th February, 1922, a violent incident occurred at Chauri Chaura in Uttar Pradesh, where a crowd set fire to a police station, resulting in the death of 22 policemen.
- Mahatma Gandhi was deeply disturbed by this outbreak of violence and believed that it violated the principle of non-violence. To prevent further bloodshed, he decided to withdraw the Non-Cooperation Movement.
- On 12th February, 1922, the Congress Working Committee formally suspended the movement at Bardoli.
- Gandhiji was arrested on 10th March, 1922 and sentenced to six years of imprisonment.

Chauri Chaura Incident

- Meanwhile, in Turkey, Kemal Pasha abolished the institution of the Caliphate and introduced radical reforms, which brought the Khilafat Movement to an end.

Impact of the Movement

- The Non-Cooperation Movement was the first nationwide mass struggle led by Mahatma Gandhi against British rule.
- It brought peasants, workers, artisans, students, traders and professionals into the national movement on a large scale.
- The Indian National Congress was transformed into a powerful mass-based organisation with a strong presence in both the urban and rural areas.
- The boycott of foreign goods encouraged the growth of Indian textile and handloom industries, while Khadi and the Charkha became symbols of self-reliance.
- The movement generated self-confidence, unity and political awareness among the Indian people.
- Gandhiji's campaign against untouchability and caste discrimination added a significant social reform dimension to Indian nationalism.
- Historian R. C. Majumdar observed that the Congress changed almost overnight from a deliberative body into a fighting organisation.
- Jawaharlal Nehru described the Non-Cooperation Movement as a 'peaceful rebellion' and a 'most civilised form of warfare'.

EXAM ORIENTED QUESTIONS

TYPE - 1

1 Mark

Multiple Choice Questions

Q.1 "It is my firm belief that we shall obtain salvation only through sufferings, not by reforms dropping on us from the English". This statement was made by Gandhiji in the context of which movement?

(a) Khilafat Movement
(b) Anti-Rowlatt Satyagraha
(c) Civil Disobedience Movement
(d) Champaran Satyagraha

Ans. (b) Anti-Rowlatt Satyagraha

Q.2 The extract given above is a report on the Jallianwala Bagh massacre, where unarmed civilians, including women and children, were fired upon by British troops.

The Statesman

13TH APRIL 1919

THE JALLIANWALA BAGH MASSACRE, ALSO KNOWN AS THE AMRITSAR MASSACRE, TOOK PLACE

On this day in 1919, British Brigadier General R.E.H. Dyer ordered his troops to open fire on the people at Jallianwala Bagh, who were protesting against the Rowlatt Act, resulting in around 1500 deaths.

Based on this report which of the following principles of justice and governance were violated by the British authorities?

P : Protection of life and liberty of citizens
Q : Fair trial and due process of law
R : Respect for civil and political rights
S : Promotion of social welfare

(a) P and Q
(b) Q and R
(c) P, Q and R
(d) R and S

Ans. (c) P, Q and R

Q.3 Which of the following events is considered to be the most significant turning point that established Gandhiji as an All-India leader?

(a) Formation of the Satyagraha Ashram in Ahmedabad.
(b) Launch of the Rowlatt Satyagraha in 1919.
(c) Jallianwala Bagh Massacre in April 1919.
(d) Suspension of the Non-Cooperation Movement in 1922.

Ans. (b) Launch of the Rowlatt Satyagraha in 1919.

Q.4 Which of the following events is considered to be the most shocking example of British brutality in Punjab, which intensified nationwide anti-British sentiment?

(a) The arrest of nationalist leaders in Punjab
(b) Martial law in Punjab
(c) Jallianwala Bagh Massacre
(d) Sale of banned literature in Punjab

Ans. (c) Jallianwala Bagh Massacre

Q.5 'A Himalayan Miscalculation'. Gandhiji used this phrase while admitting to his failure in the context of which movement?

(a) Civil Disobedience Movement
(b) Anti-Rowlatt Satyagraha
(c) Quit India Movement
(d) Khilafat Movement

Ans. (b) Anti-Rowlatt Satyagraha

Q.6 Who among the following leaders described the British colonial government as a 'Satanic Government', after the Rowlatt Act and Jallianwala Bagh massacre?

(a) Bal Gangadhar Tilak
(b) Jawaharlal Nehru
(c) Mahatma Gandhi
(d) Rabindranath Tagore

Ans. (c) Mahatma Gandhi

Q.7 Who among the following leaders formed the All-India Khilafat Committee in 1919?

(a) Abul Kalam Azad and Hakim Ajmal Khan
(b) Muhammad Ali Jinnah and Liaquat Ali Khan
(c) Shaukat Ali and Mohammad Ali
(d) Maulana Azad and Hasrat Mohani

Ans. (c) Shaukat Ali and Mohammad Ali

Q.8 Which of the following events is considered to be Gandhiji's first attempt to unite the Hindus and the Muslims in a joint political struggle?

(a) Launch of the Non-Cooperation Movement
(b) Formation of the All-India Khilafat Committee
(c) Rowlatt Satyagraha
(d) Establishment of the Satyagraha Ashram

Ans. (b) Formation of the All-India Khilafat Committee

Q.9 The following image shows Gandhiji addressing a large crowd in a public square, with people holding banners for boycott of foreign goods. Which one of the following best explains this event?

(a) A violent struggle aimed at overthrowing British rule immediately.
(b) A mass campaign of peaceful Non-Cooperation against British institutions.
(c) A demonstration supporting the Montagu-Chelmsford Reforms.
(d) A movement encouraging Indians to comply with British laws.

Ans. (b) A mass campaign of peaceful Non-Cooperation against British institutions.

Q.10 Which of the following initiatives during the Non-Cooperation Movement had goals similar to modern skill-development and self-reliance programmes?
(a) Promoting the use of Charkha and spinning yarn in villages.
(b) Launching nationwide hartals and demonstrations.
(c) Arresting protesters under martial law.
(d) Writing petitions to the British government.

Ans. (a) Promoting the use of Charkha and spinning yarn in villages.

Q.11 Identify the key difference between Rowlatt Satyagraha and the Non-Cooperation Movement.
(a) Rowlatt Satyagraha was focused on immediate independence, while Non-Cooperation Movement demanded reforms.
(b) Rowlatt Satyagraha was a short-term protest against a specific law, while Non-Cooperation Movement was a nationwide mass struggle.
(c) Non-Cooperation Movement involved violence, while Rowlatt Satyagraha was fully non-violent.
(d) Rowlatt Satyagraha was supported by all leaders of the Congress, while Non-Cooperation Movement was opposed by everyone.

Ans. (b) Rowlatt Satyagraha was a short-term protest against a specific law, while Non-Cooperation Movement was a nationwide mass struggle.

Q.12 Identify the key difference between the Khilafat Movement and the Non-Cooperation Movement.
(a) Khilafat Movement focused on protecting the Turkish Sultan, while Non-Cooperation Movement aimed at resisting British rule in India.
(b) Non-Cooperation Movement was only for Muslims, while Khilafat Movement included Hindus.
(c) Khilafat Movement encouraged violence, while Non-Cooperation Movement did not.
(d) Both movements were launched to support the British government.

Ans. (a) Khilafat Movement focused on protecting the Turkish Sultan, while Non-Cooperation Movement aimed at resisting British rule in India.

Q.13 Which violent incident led Mahatma Gandhi to suspend the Non-Cooperation Movement in 1922?
(a) Jallianwala Bagh Massacre (b) Bardoli Satyagraha
(c) Chauri Chaura Incident (d) Moplah Rebellion

Ans. (c) Chauri Chaura Incident

Q.14 'Peaceful rebellion' and 'the most civilised form of warfare.' Jawaharlal Nehru used these words to describe which movement?
(a) Khilafat Movement (b) Non-Cooperation Movement
(c) Quit India Movement (d) Swadeshi Movement

Ans. (b) Non-Cooperation Movement

Assertion-Reason Questions

Given below are two statements marked as Assertion (A) and Reason (R). Read the two statements carefully and choose the correct answer from the codes given below.

Codes
(a) Both A and R are true and R is correct explanation of A.
(b) Both A and R are true, but R is not the correct explanation of A.
(c) A is true, but R is false.
(d) Both A and R are false.

Q.1 **Assertion** (A) The Rowlatt Act of 1919 was strongly opposed by Indian nationalists.
Reason (R) The Act allowed detention without trial and denied basic civil liberties.

Ans. (c) A is true, but R is false.

Q.2 **Assertion** (A) Mahatma Gandhi described the Rowlatt Act as a law of 'No appeal, no vakil, no law'.

Reason (R) The Act provided Indians with restricted legal rights and freedom of speech.

Ans. (c) A is true, but R is false.

Q.3 **Assertion** (A) The agitation against the Rowlatt Act witnessed large-scale mass participation across India.

Reason (R) Nationwide hartals, processions, and demonstrations were organised under Gandhiji's leadership.

Ans. (a) Both A and R are true and is the correct explanation of A.

Q.4 **Assertion** (A) Rabindranath Tagore renounced his Knighthood after the Jallianwala Bagh massacre.

Reason (R) He wished to protest against British injustice and inhuman repression in Punjab.

Ans. (a) Both A and R and true and R is the correct explanation of A.

Q.5 **Assertion** (A) The Khilafat Movement helped Gandhiji expand the base of the national movement.

Reason (R) It promoted Hindu-Muslim unity by linking religious sentiments with the anti-colonial struggle.

Ans. (a) Both A and R are true and R is the correct explanation of A.

Q.6 **Assertion** (A) The Non-Cooperation Movement was formally adopted by the Congress at the Nagpur Session in 1920.

Reason (R) The Nagpur Session reorganised the Congress to transform it into a mass-based organisation.

Ans. (b) Both A and R are true, but R is not the correct explanation of A.

Very Short Answer Type Questions

Q.1 The Rowlatt Act (1919) empowered the British government to arrest people on the principle of …………….. .

Ans. Detention without trial for up to 2 years.

Q.2 The British government enforced the Rowlatt Act, granting itself powers of arrest without trial. Mahatma Gandhi responded by launching a nationwide Satyagraha. What was the significance of the Anti-Rowlatt agitation in the growth of Gandhian nationalism in India?

Ans. It marked the beginning of mass nationalism under Gandhiji and established Satyagraha as a national method of struggle against British rule.

Q.3 The image given below shows the cover page of the book 'Hind Swaraj'.

Name the author of the book 'Hind Swaraj' and the ideology it propagated against British rule in India.

Ans. Mahatma Gandhi

Q.4 On 13th April 1919, a large crowd of men, women and children gathered peacefully at Jallianwala Bagh in Amritsar to protest against the arrest of nationalist leaders. British troops opened fire on the unarmed crowd without warning.

Source: Contemporary reports on the Jallianwala Bagh massacre

State any one impact this event had on the Indian national movement.

Ans. It created nationwide anger and hatred against British rule and strengthened the demand for complete independence.

Q.5 Mention any one method adopted by Mahatma Gandhi during the Non-Cooperation Movement to oppose British rule.

Ans. One method was the boycott of government schools, law courts and foreign goods to weaken British authority through peaceful means.

Q.6 The Khilafat Movement was launched primarily to protect the principle of …………. .

Ans. Religious authority of the Khalifa

Q.7 Expand AIKC.

Ans. All-India Khilafat Committee

TYPE - 2 4 Marks

Short Answer Type Questions

Q.1 With reference to the news extract given below on the agitation against the Rowlatt Act, state any four reasons for widespread opposition in India.

IMPERIAL LEGISLATIVE COUNCIL.

BLACK BILL NO. I "PASSED."

THE HON. MR. SARMA RESIGNS.

SOLEMN MOCKERY OF THE DEBATE.

SIR WILLIAM VINCENT

Ans. The agitation against the Rowlatt Act arose due to the following reasons

- The act empowered the British government to arrest Indians without trial and detain them for up to two years.
- It denied civil liberties such as the right to appeal, legal representation and fair trial.
- Indians felt betrayed as they had expected self-government after supporting Britain during the First World War.
- The act aimed to suppress nationalist and revolutionary activities through repressive measures.

Q.2 The British government passed the Rowlatt Act in 1919, allowing detention without trial and curtailing civil liberties. Mahatma Gandhi responded by launching a nationwide Satyagraha. In the above context, analyse the impact of the Anti-Rowlatt agitation on the Indian Freedom Movement.

Ans. The Anti-Rowlatt agitation had a profound impact on the Indian freedom struggle

- It marked the beginning of mass-based political struggle under Gandhiji's leadership.
- The movement introduced Satyagraha and non-violent resistance as effective tools against colonial rule.
- It united people from different regions, classes and communities in opposition to British policies.
- Although it was partially unsuccessful in controlling British repression, it established Gandhiji as an all-India leader and inspired future nationwide movements like the Non-Cooperation Movement.

Q.3 With reference to the extract given below on the Jallianwala Bagh massacre, state any four consequences of this incident on Indian nationalism.

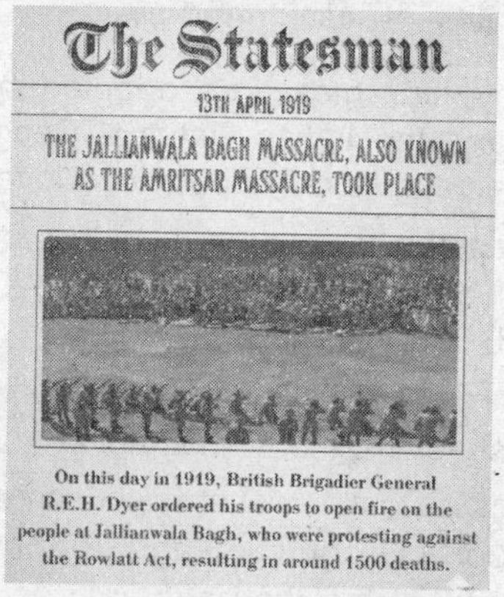
The Statesman

13TH APRIL 1919

THE JALLIANWALA BAGH MASSACRE, ALSO KNOWN AS THE AMRITSAR MASSACRE, TOOK PLACE

On this day in 1919, British Brigadier General R.E.H. Dyer ordered his troops to open fire on the people at Jallianwala Bagh, who were protesting against the Rowlatt Act, resulting in around 1500 deaths.

Ans. The Jallianwala Bagh massacre had far-reaching consequences on Indian nationalism

- It exposed the brutal and oppressive nature of British rule in India.
- It created widespread anger, fear and hatred against the colonial government.
- Rabindranath Tagore renounced his title of Knighthood in protest against British injustice.
- Gandhiji lost faith in British justice and described the government as a 'Satanic Government'.

Q.4 Discuss any four achievements of Mahatma Gandhi during the Non-Cooperation Movement that justified his emergence as a national leader of India.

Ans. Achievements of Mahatma Gandhi during the Non-Cooperation Movement were as follows

- He transformed the Indian National Congress into a mass-based organisation, bringing peasants, workers, students and professionals into the national movement.
- He popularised Satyagraha and Non-Violent resistance as effective tools against British rule.
- The boycott of foreign goods and promotion of Khadi encouraged self-reliance and boosted Indian textile and handloom industries.

- His efforts promoted Hindu-Muslim unity and social reforms, including campaigns against untouchability, strengthening the moral foundation of Indian nationalism.

Q.5 **State any four measures adopted by Mahatma Gandhi and the Indian National Congress during this movement. Non-Cooperation Movement.**

Ans. Four measures adopted by Gandhiji and the Indian National Congress of the Non-Cooperation Movement were as follows

- Mahatma Gandhi launched a nationwide hartal to protest against the Rowlatt Act.
- Indians boycotted government schools, colleges, law courts, councils and foreign goods to weaken British authority.
- The use of Khadi and the Charkha was promoted, and national schools and arbitration courts were established to encourage self-reliance.
- People were asked to renounce titles and honours conferred by the British government.

TYPE - 3 — 8 Marks

Long Answer Type Questions

Q.1 **On 1st November, 1919, the All-India Khilafat Committee adopted the programme under the guidance of Mahatma Gandhi.**

(a) Identify the movement that was linked with the Khilafat issue. State any three key objectives of this movement.

(b) Discuss any four reasons why the Khilafat Movement gained widespread support among Indian Muslims.

Ans. (a) The Non-Cooperation Movement led by Mahatma Gandhi was linked with the Khilafat issue.

Three key objectives of the movement were

(i) To protect the position of the Turkish Sultan (Khalifa) as the spiritual head of Islam.

(ii) To oppose British policies that humiliated Muslims after World War I.

(iii) To promote Hindu-Muslim unity in the fight against British colonial rule.

(b) The Khilafat Movement gained widespread support among Indian Muslims because of the following reasons

- The humiliation of the Khalifa after World War I deeply hurt the religious sentiments of Indian Muslims.
- The movement linked religious sentiments with the political struggle, making it popular among the masses.
- Mahatma Gandhi's support for the Khilafat Movement encouraged participation by Hindus and Muslims together.
- Leaders like Shaukat Ali and Mohammad Ali actively organised campaigns, spreading awareness and mobilising people across India.

Q.2 **"The Rowlatt Act of 1919 allowed the British Government to arrest people without trial, detain them for up to two years and conduct searches without warrants." With reference to this event, answer the following questions.**

(a) State any four reasons why the Rowlatt Act provoked widespread resentment in India.

(b) Discuss any two methods used by Mahatma Gandhi and his followers to protest against the Rowlatt Act and any two outcomes of the agitation.

Ans. (a) Four reasons for the widespread resentment against the Rowlatt Act are as follows

(i) It denied civil liberties by allowing arrest without trial.

(ii) It empowered the government to detain people for up to two years arbitrarily.

(iii) It allowed searches without warrants, violating privacy and rights.

(iv) Indians had supported Britain in World War I, expecting self-government, but they were instead repressed.

(b) Methods used by Mahatma Gandhi and his followers to protest against the Rowlatt Act were as follows

(i) Nationwide hartals, processions and demonstrations to show public participation.

(ii) Open defiance of banned literature, including selling books like 'Hind Swaraj' publicly.

Outcomes of the agitation

(i) Emergence of Gandhi as an all-India leader for the first time.

(ii) Widespread anger against British rule, especially after the Jallianwala Bagh massacre, boosted nationalist sentiment.

Q.3 Discuss the causes of the Non-Cooperation Movement.

Ans. The Non-Cooperation Movement was launched due to multiple reasons

- **Disappointment after World War I** Indians supported Britain with money, soldiers and loyalty, expecting the self-government, but the Montagu-Chelmsford Reforms (1919) failed to grant real autonomy.
- **Excessive War Burden** India made heavy financial contributions, including war tributes, causing widespread resentment.
- **Economic Hardship** Rising prices, inflation and scarcity of essential goods like cloth, salt and kerosene, and high taxes affected the common people.
- **Repressive British Policies Rowlatt Act (1919)** The Act allowed imprisonment without trial for up to two years and denied civil liberties.
- **Jallianwala Bagh Massacre (1919)** Brutal firing by General Dyer at the peaceful protesters in Amritsar shocked the nation and created widespread anger.
- **Khilafat Issue** The removal of the Turkish Sultan (Caliph) hurt Muslim sentiments. It provided an opportunity for Hindu-Muslim unity in the national struggle.
- **Impact of International Movements** The Bolshevik Revolution (1917) in Russia and independence movements in Ireland and Egypt inspired Indians to believe that freedom was achievable.
- **Youth Aspiration for Swaraj** Indian youth were motivated by the idea of self-rule and were willing to sacrifice for the cause of independence.

Q.4 "On 5th February 1922, a violent incident occurred at Chauri Chaura in Uttar Pradesh, where a crowd set fire to a police station, killing 22 policemen."

Source: Times of India

With reference to this event, answer the following questions.

(a) State any four reasons why Mahatma Gandhi decided to suspend the Non-Cooperation Movement.

(b) Discuss any two immediate and two long-term impacts of the suspension on Indian nationalism.

Ans. (a) Reasons for the suspension of the Non-Cooperation Movement

(i) The Chauri Chaura incident violated the principle of non-violence, which was central to Gandhiji's philosophy.

(ii) Widespread violence and lawlessness broke out in several parts of the country.

(iii) Gandhi felt that the masses were not yet trained in non-violent methods of protest.

(iv) He wanted to prevent further bloodshed and maintain moral authority of the movement.

(b) Impacts of the suspension

Two immediate impacts were

(i) The movement came to a halt, and thousands of volunteers stopped active protests.

(ii) Gandhiji observed a five-day fast and was later arrested, demonstrating accountability and moral responsibility.

Two long-term impacts were

(i) The suspension highlighted the importance of non-violence in Indian nationalist struggles.

(ii) It allowed the Indian National Congress to reorganise and plan future mass movements, laying the foundation for later campaigns like Civil Disobedience.

6

GANDHIAN NATIONALISM (1927-1937)

- The period 1927 - 1937 witnessed key events such as the Lahore Session of Congress, the declaration of Poorna Swaraj and the launch of the Civil Disobedience Movement.
- It was marked by active participation of all sections of society, including peasants, workers, women and tribal communities, in challenging British authority.
- Significant developments during this period include the Gandhi-Irwin Pact, Poona Pact and the implementation of the Government of India Act, 1935, which laid the foundation for provincial autonomy.

Nehru Report

Motilal Nehru

- In 1928, a committee under Motilal Nehru prepared the Nehru Report, which demanded Dominion Status for India within the British Empire.
- Main features of the Nehru Report
  - A responsible government with the executive accountable to an elected legislature.
  - A bicameral legislature with a Senate (200 members elected by provincial councils) and a House of Representatives (500 members elected on the basis of adult franchise).
  - Joint electorates throughout India, with limited reservations for minorities in certain provinces.
  - No communal reservations in Punjab and Bengal, and minorities in other provinces could reserve seats proportionally to their population.

Impacts of Nehru Report

- At the Calcutta Convention (December 1928), Jinnah proposed amendments (such as one-third Muslim representation at the Centre, the separation of Sind and the granting of residuary powers to provinces). These were rejected by the Hindu Mahasabha, which led Jinnah to walk out in protest.
- The rejection of his demands led Jinnah to issue the famous 'Fourteen Points' (1929), which became the basis of Muslim League's communal demands.
- Meanwhile, younger leaders like Jawaharlal Nehru and Subhas Chandra Bose opposed Dominion Status and demanded complete independence.
- Mahatma Gandhi tried to reconcile the differences within the Congress. He proposed a compromise that if the British government did not grant Dominion Status by the end of 1929, the Congress would demand complete independence.

Lahore Session

Jawaharlal Nehru

- The Lahore Session of the Indian National Congress was held in December 1929 at Lahore.
- Jawaharlal Nehru presided over the Lahore Session as the President of the Indian National Congress.
- In this session, the Congress rejected the demand for dominion status and adopted the goal of Poorna Swaraj, which meant complete independence for India.
- The Congress decided to launch the Civil Disobedience Movement if the British government failed to accept Indian demands.
- The Lahore Session marked a turning point in the national movement by clearly committing the Congress to complete independence.

Events Leading to the Lahore Session

- By the late 1920s, dissatisfaction with British rule had peaked due to the slow pace of constitutional reforms and the failure of the British government to address Indian aspirations.
- In 1927, the British government appointed the Simon Commission to review constitutional reforms in India. However, the Commission had no Indian members, which deeply offended Indian political opinion and caused widespread resentment in India.

Boycott of Simon Commission

- The Simon Commission was boycotted by the Indian National Congress, the Muslim League, Hindu Mahasabha and other political parties, and mass protests were organised across the country with the slogan "Simon Go Back."
- On 3rd February, 1928, when the Commission arrived in Bombay, a All-India hartal was observed in major cities.
- Demonstrations were met with police repression. In Lahore, Lala Lajpat Rai was injured in a lathi charge and later died, which further inflamed nationalist anger.
- Leaders like Jawaharlal Nehru and Govind Ballabh Pant also faced police brutality during protests.
- Historian Penderel Moon described the appointment of the All-White Commission as a first-class blunder, since it revived Indian nationalism at a time when the movement was losing momentum.
- The boycott forced Indian leaders to think about preparing their own constitutional framework as an alternative to British proposals.

Simon Go Back Movement

The Poorna Swaraj Resolution

- The Congress declared that complete independence (Poorna Swaraj) was the fundamental right of the Indian people of India.
- It stated that British rule in India must end because it was based on exploitation and denial of basic rights.
- The resolution rejected the idea of dominion status and all forms of British control over India.
- It affirmed that India should have full control over its political, economic and social affairs.
- The resolution emphasised the protection of civil liberties, which included freedom of speech, expression and association.
- It demanded economic independence, including control over national resources and the abolition of exploitative economic policies.
- The Congress called upon Indians to celebrate 26th January, 1930 as Independence Day to assert their right to freedom.
- It authorised the Congress Working Committee to organise mass movements, which included the Civil Disobedience Movement to achieve independence.

Civil Disobedience Movement

- The Civil Disobedience Movement (1930-1934) was a mass nationalist movement launched under the leadership of Mahatma Gandhi to challenge unjust British laws through non-violent means.
- It marked a new phase in the freedom struggle by directly involving large sections of Indian society in organised defiance of colonial authority.

Features of the Movement

- The Congress Working Committee authorised Gandhiji to launch Civil Disobedience, and he began with the historic Dandi March on 12th March, 1930.
- On 6th April, 1930, Gandhiji broke the Salt Law at Dandi, which symbolised defiance against unjust British laws.
- The programme of the movement included
  - – Violation of the Salt Law everywhere.
  - – Boycott and burning of foreign goods.
  - – Resignation of students and government servants.
  - – Refusal to pay taxes.
  - – Picketing of liquor shops.
- The movement spread rapidly across India, involving peasants, workers, women and even tribal leaders like Rani Gaidinliu of Nagaland.
- The government responded with ruthless repression: lathi charges, firing on crowds, arrests of leaders, censorship of press and confiscation of property.

Gandhiji at Dandi, broke the salt law

Gandhi-Irwin Pact

- By early 1931, the Civil Disobedience Movement had slowed due to repression and economic depression.
- Gandhiji negotiated with Viceroy Lord Irwin, which resulted in the Gandhi-Irwin Pact (5th March, 1931).
- **Main terms of the Pact**
  - – The Congress agreed to suspend Civil Disobedience Movement and participate in the Second Round Table Conference.
  - – The congress would withdraw the civil disobedience movement immediately.
  - – The Boycott of British goods would be withdrawn.
  - – Political prisoners (not charged with violence) would be released.
  - – Indians were allowed to make salt for personal use.
- The pact was approved at the Karachi Session (1931) but many leaders and peasants criticised it as a compromise.

Gandhiji and Lord Irwin

Round Table Conferences

- **First Round Table Conference** It was held in 1930. In this conference, Congress boycotted and discussions were inconclusive.
- **Second Round Table Conference** It was held in 1931 and Mahatma Gandhi attended as the sole Congress representative.This conference failed due to a communal deadlock. Muslims demanded safeguards and Dr. B.R. Ambedkar demanded separate electorates for the Depressed Classes.
- **Third Round Table Conference** It was held in 1932 and Congress boycotted again and no significant progress was made.

Second Round Table Conference

Resumption of the Movement

- After the failure of the Second Round Table Conference, Gandhiji resumed Civil Disobedience in 1932.
- The British government reacted with mass arrests, the banning of the Congress and the confiscation of property.
- The movement gradually weakened and was formally withdrawn in 1934.
- Gandhiji then shifted focus to Harijan work and rural constructive programmes.

Poona Pact

- The Poona Pact was signed in September 1932 between Mahatma Gandhi and Dr. B.R. Ambedkar.
- It was concluded to resolve the issue of separate electorates for the Depressed Classes, which had been proposed by the British government in the Communal Award.

Terms of the Poona Pact

Poona Pact

- The system of separate electorates for the Depressed Classes was abolished.
- The Depressed Classes were granted reserved seats in the provincial legislatures. These seats were to be filled through a joint electorates, not through the separate electorates.
- The number of seats reserved for the Depressed Classes was increased compared to earlier proposals.
- The Pact provided for adequate representation of the Depressed Classes in the Central Legislature. It ensured fair representation in public services for members of the Depressed Classes.
- The Pact aimed to maintain Hindu unity while protecting the political rights of the Depressed Classes.

Communal Award

Ramsay MacDonald

- The Communal Award was announced in August 1932 by the British Prime Minister Ramsay MacDonald.
- It introduced separate electorates for various communities, including Muslims, Sikhs, Christians, Anglo-Indians and the Depressed Classes.
- The Award extended the principle of communal representation, which had earlier been applied only to some religious groups.
- It proposed separate electorates for the Depressed Classes. This proposal was strongly opposed by Mahatma Gandhi.
- Gandhi believed that this provision would divide Hindu society and weaken national unity.
- In protest, Gandhi began a fast unto death while in Yeravada Jail.
- The Communal Award led directly to negotiations between Gandhi and Dr. B. R. Ambedkar. These negotiations resulted in the Poona Pact of 1932, which modified the provisions of the Communal Award.

Importance of the Movement

Women in Civil Disobedience Movement

- The Civil Disobedience Movement did not achieve Swaraj, but it clearly demonstrated the power of non-violent mass struggle under Gandhiji's leadership.
- It created a mass awakening, showing that ordinary Indians were ready to challenge the British Empire through peaceful resistance.
- The movement drew international attention, especially in the United States. Reports by foreign journalists like Webb Miller exposed the brutal repression of the British and highlighted the true nature of colonial rule.
- The participation of women and marginalised groups was on a large scale, which made the struggle more inclusive and broad-based.
- Businessmen such as Birla, Walchand Hirachand and Thakurdas supported the movement by pledging not to import foreign goods and showed the cooperation of the commercial community.
- The experience of this movement laid the foundation for the Quit India Movement of 1942, which proved that mass Satyagraha could shake the foundations of colonial rule.

Government of India Act, 1935

- The Government of India Act was passed in 1935 by the British Parliament in 1935. It was introduced and implemented by the British government under the authority of the British Parliament.
- The act was implemented to respond to growing Indian demands for greater self-government and political participation. It aimed to grant provincial autonomy and give Indian ministers more powers in the administration.
- The act also sought to establish a federal structure, which included British provinces and princely states but this federal system never came fully into effect.
- The act was the largest constitutional reform introduced before independence.
- The elections of 1937 were held under this act and revealed the growing political strength of the Congress as well as the limitations of British constitutional policies.

Main Features of the Act

- **Provincial Autonomy** The provinces were given elected governments with more powers and ended dyarchy at the provincial level.
- **Federal Structure** A federation was planned, which included British provinces and princely states but it never materialised because princely states did not join.
- **Dyarchy at the Centre** The dyarchy was abolished at the provincial level and introduced at the centre.
- **Separate Electorates** Separate Electorates were extended to minorities, women and labour, which further deepened communal divisions.
- **Franchise Expansion** Franchise was expanded to about 10% of the population was enfranchised, but voting rights remained limited.
- **Federal Court** A Federal court was established to settle disputes between provinces and the Centre.

Elections of 1937

- Elections were held in 1937 under the provisions of the 1935 Act.
- The Congress formed government in 8 provinces. U.P., Bihar, Bombay, Madras, Central Provinces, Orissa, Assam and North-West Frontier Province.
- The elections demonstrated that the Congress was the dominant political force and communal divisions and regional politics persisted.

Main Developments under Congress Ministries

- The Congress ministries introduced significant educational reforms by expanding primary education, promoting the use of vernacular languages, and encouraging national culture in schools and colleges.
- In the field of agriculture, Congress governments provided relief to peasants by reducing land revenue in some provinces, introducing tenancy reforms and protecting cultivators from exploitation by landlords.
- Labour welfare was improved through better working conditions, recognition of trade unions and the introduction of legislation aimed at safeguarding workers' rights.
- Civil liberties were strengthened as Congress ministries relaxed press restrictions, released political prisoners and encouraged the growth of local self-government institutions.
- Social reforms were promoted through the encouragement of khadi, implementation of prohibition campaigns and efforts towards the upliftment of Harijans.

Main Developments under Non-Congress Ministries

- In Punjab, the Unionist Party led by Sir Sikandar Hayat Khan focused on peasant welfare while attempting to maintain communal harmony among different religious communities.
- In Bengal, the Krishak Praja Party under A.K. Fazlul Huq emphasised agrarian reforms and peasant interests, though the ministry suffered from political instability.
- In Sind, regional leaders faced difficulties due to factional politics and rising communal tensions.
- Overall, non-Congress ministries lacked a unified national vision and were largely dependent on coalition politics, which limited their effectiveness.

Sir Sikandar hayat Khan

A.K. Fazlul Huq

EXAM ORIENTED QUESTIONS

TYPE - 1   1 Mark

Multiple Choice Questions

Q.1 Which of the following events is considered the most significant protest against the lack of Indian representation in the British government?

(a) The Dandi March and breaking of the Salt Law in 1930.

(b) The Simon Commission boycott of 1928.

(c) The signing of the Gandhi–Irwin Pact in 1931.

(d) The Poona Pact of 1932.

Ans. (b) The Simon Commission boycott of 1928.

Q.2 Identify the key difference between Dominion Status and Poorna Swaraj.

(a) Dominion Status demanded complete independence, while Poorna Swaraj accepted British sovereignty.

(b) Dominion Status aimed at self-government within the British Empire, while Poorna Swaraj demanded complete independence.

(c) Poorna Swaraj was proposed by the British government, while Dominion Status was proposed by the Congress.

(d) Both aimed at the same political objective.

Ans. (b) Dominion Status aimed at self-government within the British Empire, while Poorna Swaraj demanded complete independence.

Q.3 "On 31st December 1929, Jawaharlal Nehru hoisted the tricolour flag on the banks of the River Ravi, and the Congress declared complete independence as its goal."

Identify the resolution associated with this historic event.

(a) Dominion Status Resolution

(b) Nehru Report Resolution

(c) Poorna Swaraj Resolution

(d) Civil Disobedience Resolution

Ans. (c) Poorna Swaraj Resolution

Q.4 "On 12th March 1930, Mahatma Gandhi began a historic march from Sabarmati Ashram to the coastal village of Dandi to challenge an unjust colonial law."

Identify the law that was deliberately violated through this action.

(a) Forest Law   (b) Rowlatt Act

(c) Salt Law   (d) Vernacular Press Act

Ans. (c) Salt Law

Q.5 Which of the following events is considered to be the high point of Gandhiji's political influence during the Civil Disobedience Movement?

(a) The Simon Commission boycott of 1928.

(b) The Dandi March and breaking of the Salt Law in 1930.

(c) The signing of the Gandhi–Irwin Pact in 1931.

(d) The Poona Pact of 1932.

Ans. (b) The Dandi March and breaking of the Salt Law in 1930

Q.6 The following is an image of Mahatma Gandhi breaking the Salt Law at Dandi during the Civil Disobedience Movement (1930). Which one of the following best explains the significance of this act in the nationalist movement?

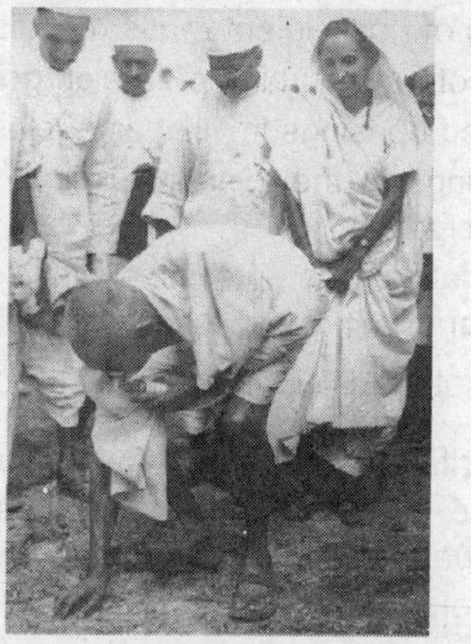

(a) It symbolised organised non-violent defiance of unjust British laws and mobilised the masses.

(b) It marked the end of constitutional reforms under British rule.

(c) It was aimed only at addressing economic grievances of salt manufacturers.

(d) It led to the immediate grant of complete independence.

Ans. (a) It symbolised organised non-violent defiance of unjust British laws and mobilised the masses.

Q.7 The extract given below refers to the Civil Disobedience Movement launched by Mahatma Gandhi in 1930, marked by the breaking of the Salt Law at Dandi. Which of the following principles of Gandhian nationalism were applied during this movement?

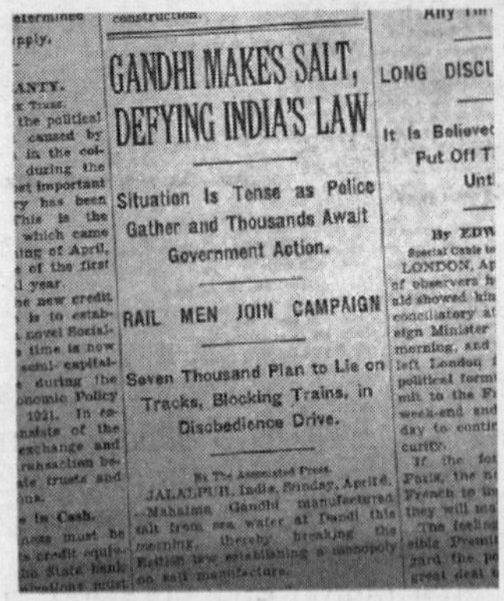
GANDHI MAKES SALT, DEFYING INDIA'S LAW

Situation Is Tense as Police Gather and Thousands Await Government Action.

RAIL MEN JOIN CAMPAIGN

Seven Thousand Plan to Lie on Tracks, Blocking Trains, in Disobedience Drive.

By The Associated Press.

JALALPUR, India, Sunday, April 6. —Mahatma Gandhi manufactured salt from sea water at Dandi this morning, thereby breaking the British law establishing a monopoly on salt manufacture.

P : Non-violent resistance

Q : Participation of peasants, women, and workers

R : Armed rebellion against British authority

S : Moral pressure on the colonial government

(a) P and Q (b) R and S

(c) P, Q and S (d) Q and R

Ans. (c) P, Q and S

Q.8 Which of the following actions during the Civil Disobedience Movement similar to Gandhiji's principle of non-violent mass mobilisation?

(a) Boycott and burning of foreign goods across India.

(b) Armed uprisings in villages against British officials.

(c) Signing of the Gandhi–Irwin Pact without public participation.

(d) Formation of provincial ministries under the Government of India Act.

Ans. (a) Boycott and burning of foreign goods across India.

Q.9 "The British Communal Award of 1932 proposed separate electorates for the Depressed Classes, which was strongly opposed by a leader and he undertook a fast."

Who among the following leaders signed an agreement with Dr. B.R. Ambedkar to resolve this issue?

(a) Jawaharlal Nehru

(b) Lord Irwin

(c) Mahatma Gandhi

(d) Madan Mohan Malaviya

Ans. (c) Mahatma Gandhi

Q.10 Which of the following events is considered the key compromise that prevented division within Hindu society while addressing the rights of Depressed Classes?

(a) Gandhi-Irwin Pact, 1931

(b) Poona Pact, 1932

(c) Nehru Report, 1928

(d) Lahore Session Resolution, 1929

Ans. (b) Poona Pact, 1932

Q.11 Which of the following initiatives during the 1937 Congress ministries reflects goals similar to Gandhiji's focus on rural development?

(a) Reduction of land revenue and protection of tenants' rights.

(b) Promotion of English-language education in cities.

(c) Formation of coalitions with non-Congress ministries.

(d) Expanding separate electorates for minorities.

Ans. (a) Reduction of land revenue and protection of tenants' rights.

Q.12 Which of the following developments best demonstrated the growing political strength of the Indian National Congress before independence?

(a) Participation in the First Round Table Conference, 1930.

(b) Winning a majority in the 1937 provincial elections under the Government of India Act.

(c) Signing the Gandhi-Irwin Pact, 1931.

(d) Boycott of the Simon Commission, 1928.

Ans. (b) Winning a majority in the 1937 provincial elections under the Government of India Act.

Assertion - Reason Questions

Given below are two statements marked as Assertion (A) are Reason (R). Read the two statements carefully and choose the correct answer from the codes given below.

(a) Both A and R are true and R is the correct explanation of A.

(b) Both A and R are true but R is not the correct explanation of A.

(c) A is true, but R is false.

(d) Both A and R are false.

Q.1 Assertion (A) The Simon Commission was boycotted by Indian political parties.

Reason (R) The Commission included three British members and one Indian representative.

Ans. (c) A is true and R is false.

Q.2 Assertion (A) Young leaders like Jawaharlal Nehru and Subhas Chandra Bose opposed Dominion Status.

Reason (R) They believed that only complete independence could fulfill India's aspirations.

Ans. (a) Both A and R are true and R is the correct explanation of A.

Q.3 Assertion (A) The Lahore Session of Congress in declared Dominion Status as its ultimate goal.

Reason (R) The British government accepted India's demand for Dominion Status, so Congress could demand complete independence.

Ans. (d) Both A and R are false.

Q.4 **Assertion** (A) The Dandi March of 1932 marked the beginning of the Civil Disobedience Movement.

Reason (R) Jawaharlal Nehru led the march to break the Salt Law as a symbolic act of non-violent resistance.

Ans. (d) Both A and R are false.

Q.5 **Assertion** (A) The Gandhi–Irwin Pact led to the suspension of the Civil Disobedience Movement.

Reason (R) The Pact allowed Indians to make salt for personal use and released certain political prisoners.

Ans. (a) Both A and R are true and R is the correct explanation of A.

Q.6 **Assertion** (A) The Poona Pact ensured reserved representation for Depressed Classes in joint electorates.

Reason (R) Gandhiji opposed the separate electorates granted by the British Communal Award of 1934.

Ans. (c) A is true, but R is false.

Q.7 **Assertion (A)** Congress ministries introduced educational and agrarian reforms after the 1937 elections.

Reason (R) The Government of India Act, 1935 gave provincial autonomy to elected governments.

Ans. (a) Both A and R are true and R is the correct explanation of A.

Very Short Answer Type Questions

Q.1 The .... of the Indian National Congress in 1929 adopted Poorna Swaraj as its ultimate goal.

Ans. Lahore Session

Q.2 Expand INC.

Ans. Indian National Congress

Q.3 The image given below shows Mahatma Gandhi leading a march to the coastal village of. Dandi in 1930.

Name the movement referred to in the image.

Ans. Civil Disobedience Movement

Q.4 "On 12th March, 1930, Mahatma Gandhi began a march from Sabarmati Ashram to Dandi to break the Salt Law and challenge British authority."

State any one impact this event had on the Indian freedom struggle.

Ans. This event marked the beginning of the Civil Disobedience Movement, mobilised large sections of Indian society, drew international attention, and demonstrated the power of non-violent mass resistance against British rule.

Q.5 Mention any one provision of the Gandhi–Irwin Pact of 1931 that impacted the Indian freedom struggle.

Ans. It allowed the release of non-violent political prisoners.

Q.6

In the picture shown above, Mahatma Gandhi can be seen participating in the .... Conference in London, in 1931, representing the Indian National Congress to negotiate with the British Government regarding India's constitutional reforms.

Ans. Second Round Table

Q.7 "The Poona Pact was signed in 1932 between Mahatma Gandhi and Dr. B.R. Ambedkar." What was the importance of this event for Indian society?

Ans. The Poona Pact ensured reserved representation for the Depressed Classes in joint electorates, prevented division within the Hindu society.

Q.8 The Government of India Act, 1935 granted .... to provinces, ending dyarchy at the provincial level.

Ans. provincial autonomy

Q.9 The provincial elections held in 1937 under the Government of India Act, 1935 demonstrated the political dominance of .... in India.

Ans. Indian National Congress

TYPE - 2 — 4 Marks

Short Answer Type Questions

Q.1 "The Simon Commission, appointed in 1927 without any Indian members, faced nationwide protests and was boycotted by the Congress, the Muslim League and other parties." In the above context, analyse the significance of the Simon Commission boycott in shaping India's nationalist movement.

Ans. The significance of the Simon Commission boycott in shaping India's nationalist movement was

- The boycott united various political parties and communities, including Congress, Muslim League, and Hindu Mahasabha, against British policies. It revived nationalist sentiment at a time when the freedom movement had slowed down.
- The protests led to the drafting of the Nehru Report, which proposed Dominion Status as an Indian alternative to British constitutional reforms.
- Leaders like Lala Lajpat Rai, Jawaharlal Nehru, and Subhas Chandra Bose emerged as prominent figures in mass mobilisations.
- The movement strengthened the demand for complete independence and set the stage for future mass movements led by Gandhi.

Q.2 "The Civil Disobedience Movement (1930–1934) involved peasants, workers, women, students and tribal leaders in organised defiance of British laws, including the boycott of foreign goods and refusal to pay taxes." Based on the above report, state any four reasons for the Civil Disobedience Movement.

Ans. Four reasons for the Civil Disobedience Movement are

(i) The illegitimacy of British rule in India and oppressive colonial policies created widespread resentment among Indians.

(ii) The failure of the British government to grant meaningful constitutional reforms and respond to Indian political demands prompted the need for direct action.

(iii) The imposition of unjust laws, such as the Salt Tax, symbolised the economic exploitation of Indians, motivating the defiance.

(iv) There was a desire to mobilise ordinary citizens, including peasants, workers, women and students, in a non-violent struggle to awaken national consciousness and unity against colonial rule.

Q.3 With reference to the news extract given below, state any four circumstances that contributed to the success and nationwide impact of the Civil Disobedience Movement.

The Tribune.

VOL. LI. NO. 70 — LAHORE, WEDNESDAY, MARCH 25, 1930. — Price One Anna

GANDHI DECLARES NATIONWIDE NON-VIOLENT SALT MARCH.

CONGRESS RELAUNCHES ITS NON-COOPERATION CAMPAIGN

PEACEFUL PROTEST AGAINST UNFAIR SALT LAWS

OPPOSITION AND DISREGARD OF BRITISH POLICIES

Mass chaos ensues in India as Mahatma Gandhi leads another non-cooperation campaign against the British.

The Congress has been firm in its attempts to slacken the crown's hold on India, the march being a continuation of non-cooperation caused by immense opposition to the Simon Commission and the British rejection of the Nehru Report.

GANDHI LEADING THE MARCH.

The focal point of the march is apparently an attack on Britain's unfair salt laws in India. The British's lucrative trade of salt was a direct result of the prohibition of Indian use of its own salt resources, now being protested against.

JINNAH CONDEMNS SALT MARCH DUE TO THREAT OF HINDU DOMINANCE

Mohammed Ali Jinnah has proved to be a great Muslim political leader by disapproving of the Salt March. It is a great risk to Muslims, as they would be threatened from both sides if the mistake of joining the march is made.

The Congress has no intention of allowing the Muslims a separate electorate, putting their security further at risk. This is evident from the Nehru Report, as it presented the idea of no separate electorates for minorities and the Congress failed to accept Jinnah's proposals on behalf of the Muslims which enabled them to have a say in the central and provincial councils and protect themselves from Hindu oppression. Jinnah described this as the "parting of the ways" as it was now certain that the Congress failed to recognise the need to cooperate with the League and consider it a representative of the Indian Muslim population.

Ans. Four circumstances that contributed to the success and nationwide impact of the Civil Disobedience Movement are

(i) Massive participation of diverse sections of society, including peasants, women, students and tribal leaders.

(ii) Non-violent methods like boycott of foreign goods, refusal to pay taxes and picketing liquor shops.

(iii) Widespread international attention highlighting British repression and moral illegitimacy of colonial rule.

(iv) Leadership of Mahatma Gandhi and the organisational support of the Indian National Congress, which inspired mass mobilisation.

Q.4 Discuss any four achievements of Mahatma Gandhi through the Gandhi-Irwin Pact that justify its significance in India's freedom struggle.

Ans. Four achievements of Mahatma Gandhi through the Gandhi–Irwin pact that justify its significance in India's freedom struggle are

(i) It led to the release of political prisoners who were not charged with acts of violence, which boosted morale among freedom fighters.

(ii) It permitted Indians to produce and use salt for personal purposes, symbolically undermining British authority.

(iii) The Pact temporarily suspended the Civil Disobedience Movement, showing that peaceful negotiations could achieve tangible results.

(iv) It enabled Congress to participate in the Second Round Table Conference in London, giving India a voice in constitutional discussions.

Q.5 "The Poona Pact was signed in 1932 between Mahatma Gandhi and Dr. B.R. Ambedkar regarding the representation of Depressed Classes in India." Discuss any four achievements of the Poona Pact that highlight its importance in Indian social and political history.

Ans. Four achievements of the Poona Pact that highlight its importance in Indian social and political history are

(i) It ensured reserved seats for the Depressed Classes in joint electorates, replacing the separate electorates proposed by the British Communal Award.

(ii) It avoided division within Hindu society by integrating representation in a joint system.

(iii) The Pact strengthened the political voice of marginalised communities, giving them an opportunity to participate in governance.

(iv) It set a precedent for negotiated reforms through dialogue rather than conflict, reinforcing non-violent methods in social and political struggles.

Q.6 State any four key reforms introduced by the Congress ministries after the 1937 elections.

Ans. Four key reforms introduced by the Congress ministries after the 1937 elections are

(i) **Educational Reforms** Expanded primary education, promoted vernacular or regional languages, and encouraged national culture in schools and colleges.

(ii) **Agricultural Reforms** Reduced land revenue, introduced tenancy reforms, and protected cultivators from landlord exploitation.

(iii) **Labour Welfare** Improved working conditions, recognised trade unions, and introduced legislation safeguarding workers' rights.

(iv) **Civil Liberties and Social Reforms** Relaxed press restrictions, released political prisoners, promoted khadi, implemented prohibition campaigns and worked for the upliftment of Harijans or Socio-economic advancement of Harijans.

Q.7 State any four challenges faced by the Non-Congress ministries in the provinces.

Ans. Four challenges faced by the Non-Congress ministries in the provinces are

(i) **Political Instability** The ministry of the Krishak Praja Party in Bengal struggled due to factionalism.

(ii) **Communal Tensions** Leaders in Punjab and Sindh had to manage rising conflicts between religious communities.

(iii) **Lack of Unified Vision** Non-Congress ministries were largely coalition-based and lacked a national strategy.

(iv) **Limited Effectiveness in Reforms** Regional politics and divisions hampered the implementation of social and economic reforms.

TYPE - 3   8 Marks

Long Answer Type Questions

Q.1 "The Indian National Congress, in December 1929, declared 'Poorna Swaraj' as its ultimate goal and resolved to celebrate 26th January, 1930 as Independence Day."

(a) Identify the session of the Indian National Congress referred to in the extract. State any three decisions taken during this session.

(b) Discuss any four reasons why the Session was a turning point in India's freedom struggle.

Ans. (a) The session of the Indian National Congress was the Lahore Session, December 1929. The three decisions taken during this session were

(i) Declaration of Poorna Swaraj (Complete Independence) as the ultimate goal of Congress.

(ii) Decision to launch Civil Disobedience Movement if the British government refused to grant independence.

(iii) 26th January, 1930 was to be observed as the first Independence Day across India.

(b) The Lahore Session became a turning point in India's freedom struggle because

(i) It marked a shift from Dominion Status to Poorna Swaraj as the nationalist goal.

(ii) It mobilised the masses across India, including peasants, workers, women and students.

(iii) It symbolised the rise of a younger generation of leaders, such as Jawaharlal Nehru, who presided over the session.

(iv) It set the stage for nationwide mass movements, including the Civil Disobedience Movement led by Mahatma Gandhi.

Q.2 "On 12th March 1930, Mahatma Gandhi began the Dandi March to defy the Salt Law and challenge British authority, which spread into a nationwide Civil Disobedience Movement." With reference to the Civil Disobedience Movement (1930–1934), answer the following questions.

(a) State any four key features of the Civil Disobedience Movement.

(b) Discuss any two reasons, each for the widespread participation of Indians and the limited success of the movement in achieving immediate independence.

Ans. Four key features of the Civil Disobedience Movement are

(i) Non-violent defiance of unjust British laws, led by Mahatma Gandhi.

(ii) Dandi March and breaking of the Salt Law as a symbolic act of resistance.

(iii) Boycott of foreign goods, picketing of liquor shops and refusal to pay taxes as part of nationwide participation.

(iv) Mass participation of diverse sections of society, including peasants, workers, women, students and tribal leaders.

(b) Two reasons for the widespread participation of Indians are

(i) Non-violent methods encouraged participation from ordinary people who feared violence less.

(ii) The leadership of Gandhi and the organisational support of Congress inspired mass mobilisation across the country.

Two reasons for the limited success of the movement in achieving immediate independence are

(i) The British Government responded with repression, arrests and censorship, limiting immediate impact.

(ii) The movement was temporarily suspended due to negotiations like the Gandhi-Irwin Pact, preventing complete success.

Q.3 Discuss any eight features of the Government of India Act, 1935.

Ans. Eight features of the Government of India Act, 1935 are

(i) **Provincial Autonomy** Provinces were given elected governments with more powers and dyarchy was abolished at the provincial level.

(ii) **Federal Structure** A federation comprising British provinces and the princely states was proposed, though it never materialised because the princely states did not join.

(iii) **Dyarchy at the Centre** the Dyarchy was introduced at the central level, with certain areas under British control.

(iv) **Separate Electorates** Extended to minorities, women and labour, which reinforced communal divisions.

(v) **Franchise Expansion** About 10% of the population gained voting rights, though the franchise remained limited.

(vi) **Federal Court** Established to settle disputes between the provinces and the Centre.

(vii) **Provisions for Provincial Elections** Allowed elections and formation of Congress ministries in several provinces in 1937.

(viii) **Legislative Powers** Introduced bicameral legislatures at the Centre and unicameral legislatures in the provinces, giving Indians some experience in governance.

World History

7

WORLD WAR I

- World War I (1914–1918) was a global war caused by Alliances, Imperialism, Militarism, Nationalism and the assassination of Archduke Franz Ferdinand.
- It turned Europe into an armed camp and led to major changes in maps and politics.

Long-Term Causes of World War I

Alliance System

- The alliance system divided Europe into two armed camps which were the Triple Alliance and the Triple Entente, which made peace weak and unstable.
- Countries believed that forming alliances would protect them, but these alliances increased fear and tension among nations.
- In 1879, Germany and Austria-Hungary signed the Dual Alliance to support each other in case of war. Later, Italy joined Germany and Austria-Hungary, and together they formed the Triple Alliance.
- The Triple Alliance followed a defensive policy under Bismarck to maintain peace in Europe. However, when Kaiser William II came to power, the Triple Alliance became aggressive in nature.
- In response to this, Britain, France and Russia signed a series of agreements between 1894 and 1907. These agreements led to the formation of the Triple Entente.

Kaiser William II

- As a result, Germany felt surrounded by France and Russia on land and challenged by Britain and France at sea.

Imperialism

- Imperialism is a political system in which a rich and powerful country, nation exerts control over weaker territories (colonies) to exploit their resources and labour.
- European nations competed with each other to acquire colonies in Africa and Asia. This competition created rivalry among powerful countries like Britain, France and Germany.
- Germany wanted more colonies, but it had fewer colonies compared to Britain and France.
- German Emperor Kaiser William II, openly expressed German anger by saying that most colonies belonged to Britain and France, while Germany also deserved its share.
- The struggle for colonies increased tensions and distrust among European powers and helped create the conditions for the First World War.

Interpretations on Imperialism

- Marxist historians believed that imperialism was the highest stage of capitalism, where countries were forced to expand outside their borders.
- **J. A. Hobson** explained that rich capitalists pushed governments to capture colonies for cheap raw materials and new markets.
- **Vladimir Lenin** argued that imperialism was unavoidable under capitalism because industrialists constantly sought for higher profits abroad.

Militarism (Arms Race)

- European nations believed that strong armies and navies were necessary for national security.
- Britain considered naval supremacy essential for its survival.
- Germany expanded its navy under Admiral Tirpitz to challenge Britain's dominance at sea. To strengthen its navy, Germany deepened the Kiel Canal so that battleships could move easily.
- At the same time, France renewed its laws and made military service compulsory for men aged 26 to 48.
- Russia also increased the size of its army, even though its economy was weak.
- Belgium expanded its army by providing funds through parliamentary grants.
- New weapons such as torpedoes, torpedo boats and destroyers were developed, making warfare more deadly.
- By 1900, Europe had become an Armed continent, where militarism strongly influenced politics and diplomacy.

Nationalism

- Nationalism encouraged people to glorify their own nation and often created hatred towards other nations.
- In Germany, historians like Siebel, Treitschke and Philosophers like Bernhard, promoted the doctrine of superiority of the Teutonic race (ancient tribe of Germany).
- Similarly, in England, writers like Homer Lea promoted Anglo-Saxon superiority (Superiority of English-speaking peoples).

Treitschke

Homer Lea

- In France, nationalism took the form of revenge because the country wanted to recover the Alsace and Lorraine regions which they had lost to Germany in 1870. Therefore, France actively looked for allies against Germany.
- Nationalism was also strong in the Balkan region and became a major cause of tension because
  - Serbia wanted to unite all Slavic people into one independent state.
  - Austria-Hungary opposed Serbian ambitions because it feared losing control over the region of Bosnia and Herzegovina.
  - Russia supported Serbia because it considered itself the protector of the Slavic people.
  - As a result, rivalries developed in the Balkans, including Austro-Serbian, Serbo-Bulgarian and Austro-Russian conflicts.
- Pan-Germanism aimed to unite all German-speaking people, while Pan-Slavism aimed to unite all Slavs. These opposing ideologies led to diplomatic friction and conflict between European powers.
- Nationalism made people view war as a moral duty and made peaceful compromise very difficult.
- The assassination of Archduke Franz Ferdinand in 1914, was the most extreme example of nationalist violence and became the immediate cause of the First World War.

Main Short-Term Causes (Events from 1908–1914)

- In 1908, Austria-Hungary annexed Bosnia-Herzegovina, which angered Serbia and Russia and increased tension among the European powers.
- The assassination (murder) of Archduke Franz Ferdinand of Austria in Sarajevo by a Serbian nationalist in June 1914 was the immediate cause of the First World War, because it led Austria-Hungary to declare war on Serbia, which then activated the alliance system and turned a local conflict into a world war.

Paris Peace Settlements

- The Paris Peace Settlements were a series of treaties signed after the end of the First World War between 1919-1920 to reorganise Europe and maintain peace.
- These settlements aimed to punish the defeated powers and redraw national boundaries according to the principle of nationalism. However, this principle was not applied equally, which created new problems and tensions.

Paris Peace Settlements (1919-1920)

REVISION NOTES

Changes in the Map of Europe

Division of Austria-Hungary The Austro-Hungarian Empire was divided into several independent states- Austria, Hungary, Czechoslovakia and Yugoslavia to satisfy the demands of different nationalities living under the empire.

Disintegration of the Ottoman Empire The Ottoman Empire lost most of its territories. Turkey survived as an independent state, but its Arab provinces were taken away by Britain and France and it ended the Ottoman control outside Anatolia.

Territorial Losses of Germany Germany was severely reduced in size. It returned Alsace-Lorraine to France, lost territories to Belgium and Denmark, and large areas were transferred to Poland and it weakened Germany both strategically and economically.

TREATY SIGNED; WAR OVER

The Evening World. FINAL

WILSON LEAVES PARIS; SAILS SUNDAY

GERMANS PLEDGED TO ACT IN GOOD FAITH

TREATY SEVERE ON GERMANY, SAYS WILSON, BUT IMPOSES NOTHING SHE CANNOT DO

GUNS BOOM, PLANES FILL AIR; FRENCH CROWDS CHEER PEACE

Re-creation of Poland Poland was re-established as an independent nation after more than a century. It was formed from territories taken from Germany, Austria-Hungary, and Russia and gave Poland access to the sea through the Polish Corridor.

Emergence of New States from Russia Several small independent states such as Finland, Latvia, Lithuania and Estonia emerged from former Russian territories, and reduced Russian influence in Eastern Europe.

oblems Created by the New Map

he map of Europe was redrawn on the principle of nationalism but it was applied unevenly. Many newly formed ates contained mixed ethnic and linguistic groups, which led to minority problems, internal tensions and political stability.

reaty of Versailles

The Treaty of Versailles was signed on 28th June, 1919 between the Allied Powers and Germany.

It officially ended the First World War and imposed harsh political, territorial, military and economic terms on Germany.

Germany was held solely responsible for causing the war under Article 231, which justified the severe punishments imposed on it.

itical evaluation of the Treaty of Versailles

Harsh Nature The treaty imposed extremely severe terms on Germany. The War Guilt Clause humiliated Germany and placed sole responsibility for the war on the German nation, which created anger and resentment among the German people.

Economic Weakness of Germany Heavy war reparations destroyed the German economy, which led to nflation, unemployment and widespread poverty. This economic instability undermined democratic government n Germany.

Unfair Territorial Settlements Germany lost important industrial and strategic territories. The creation of new states and boundaries ignored ethnic realities and left many Germans outside Germany and caused minority problems.

Failure to Apply Nationalism Consistently Although the principle of nationalism was promoted but this principle was not applied uniformly. Many new states had mixed populations, which led to political instability and future conflicts in Europe.

Absence of Key Powers The Treaty was mainly framed by Britain and France without Germany's participation. As Germany was excluded from the negotiations, it created deep hostility, aggression and resentment . At the ame time, the United States refused to accept the Treaty, which weakened its authority and made it less ffective in maintaining peace.

Weakness of the League of Nations The League of Nations, created by the treaty, lacked a military force of its wn and the support of major powers, making it ineffective in maintaining peace.

REVISION NOTES

EXAM ORIENTED QUESTIONS

TYPE - 1 — 1 Mark

Multiple Choice Questions

Q.1 Identify the key feature of the Triple Alliance during the period of Bismarck.

(a) It was aggressive and expansionist in nature.
(b) It was defensive and aimed at preserving peace.
(c) It included Britain as a major naval power.
(d) It was formed to oppose the Ottoman Empire.

Ans. (b) It was defensive and aimed at preserving peace.

Q.2 "Wherever I look in the world, it is either a British or a French colony. Germany too lives under the Sun."-

Kaiser William II

The statement reflects Germany's resentment mainly due to

(a) the spread of nationalism in the Balkans.
(b) the unequal distribution of colonies among European powers.
(c) the military alliance between Britain and France.
(d) the decline of the Ottoman Empire.

Ans. (b) the unequal distribution of colonies among European powers.

Q.3 Identify the immediate cause of the First World War.

(a) Annexation of Bosnia-Herzegovina
(b) Balkan Wars
(c) Arms race in Europe
(d) Assassination of Archduke Franz Ferdinand

Ans. (d) Assassination of Archduke Franz Ferdinand

Q.4 The following refers to the Paris Peace Settlements (1919–1920), which redrew the political map of Europe after the First World War. Which one of the following best explains a major problem created by these settlements?

(a) All nationalities were successfully given separat nation-states.
(b) The principle of nationalism was applied unevenly creating minority problems.
(c) Europe achieved long-term political stability.
(d) The settlements eliminated future causes of conflic

Ans. (b) The principle of nationalism was applied unevenly creating minority problems.

Q.5 The extract given below refers to the Paris Peac Settlements (1919–1920), which aimed to reorganis Europe after the First World War. Which of th following principles was most clearly violated by th Paris Peace Settlements?

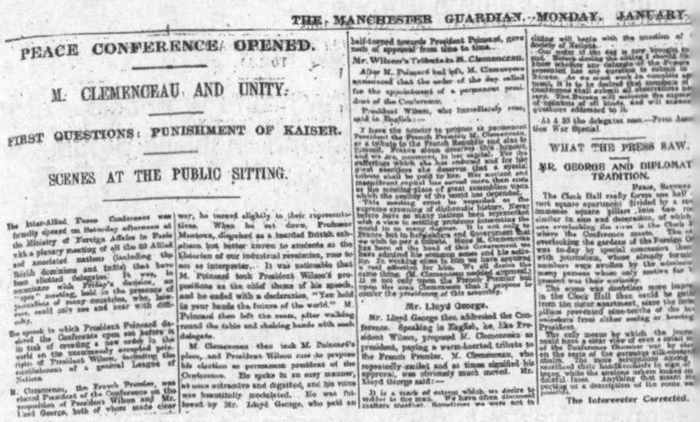

THE MANCHESTER GUARDIAN, MONDAY, JANUARY

PEACE CONFERENCE OPENED.

M. CLEMENCEAU AND UNITY.

FIRST QUESTIONS: PUNISHMENT OF KAISER.

SCENES AT THE PUBLIC SITTING.

Mr. Wilson's Tribute to M. Clemenceau.

Mr. Lloyd George.

WHAT THE PRESS SAW.

MR. GEORGE AND DIPLOMAT TRADITION.

P : The consistent application of the principle nationalism
Q : Fair treatment of defeated nations
R : Creation of ethnically homogeneo nation-states
S : Long-term political stability in Europe

(a) P and Q (b) Q and R
(c) P and R (d) P and S

Ans. (c) P and R

Q.6 Identify the key difference between the Paris Pea Settlements and the Treaty of Versailles.

(a) The Paris Peace Settlements dealt only w Germany, while the Treaty of Versailles dealt with defeated powers.
(b) The Paris Peace Settlements were a series of treat with different defeated powers, while the Treaty Versailles was specifically signed with Germany.
(c) The Treaty of Versailles was signed before the Pa Peace Settlements began.
(d) The Treaty of Versailles focused on territo changes only, while the Paris Peace Settleme focused only on military terms.

Ans. (b) The Paris Peace Settlements were a series of treaties with different defeated powers, while the Treaty of Versailles was specifically signed with Germany.

Q.7 Which of the following treaties formally ended the First World War and imposed harsh terms on Germany?

(a) Treaty of Vienna (b) Treaty of Frankfurt
(c) Treaty of Versailles (d) Treaty of Trianon

Ans. (c) Treaty of Versailles

Q.8 "The War Guilt Clause humiliated Germany and placed sole responsibility for the war on it." -

Treaty of Versailles

The clause mentioned above mainly resulted in

(a) strengthening of democratic institutions in Germany.
(b) economic stability and political peace in Europe.
(c) anger and resentment among the German people.
(d) immediate success of the League of Nations.

Ans. (c) anger and resentment among the German people.

Assertion-Reason Questions

Given below are two statements marked as Assertion (A) and Reason (R). Read the two statements carefully and choose the correct answer from the codes given below.

(a) Both A and R are true and R is the correct explanation of A.
(b) Both A and R are true but R is not the correct explanation of A.
(c) A is true, but R is false.
(d) Both A and R are false.

Q.1 Assertion (A) The alliance system made Europe politically unstable before 1914.

Reason (R) Rival alliances ensured that a local conflict could quickly involve many countries.

Ans. (a) Both A and R are true and R is the correct explanation of A.

Q.2 Assertion (A) Germany felt 'encircled' by hostile powers before the First World War.

Reason (R) France and Russia formed a land-based alliance while Britain dominated the seas.

Ans. (a) Both A and R are true and R is the correct explanation of A.

Q.3 Assertion (A) Militarism contributed to the outbreak of the First World War.

Reason (R) European nations did not glorify military power.

Ans. (c) A is true, but R is false.

Q.4 Assertion (A) The League of Nations was ineffective in maintaining international peace.

Reason (R) The League of Nations encouraged secret diplomacy among European powers.

Ans. (c) A is true, but R is false.

Very Short Answer Type Questions

Q.1 The alliance between Germany and Austria-Hungary signed in 1879 was known as the ....

Ans. Dual Alliance

Q.2 The crisis that arose due to German opposition to French claims in Morocco in 1911 was the .... Crisis.

Ans. Agadir

Q.3 Expand PPS.

Ans. Paris Peace Settlements.

Q.4 The Paris Peace Settlements attempted to redraw the map of Europe on the principle of ....

Ans. Nationalism or self-determination

Q.5 The photograph shows the creation of the League of Nations after World War I. *(Source:Wikipedia)*

Name the international organisation established by the Paris Peace Settlements to maintain peace.

Ans. League of Nations

Q.6 Mention any one provision of the League of Nations that was intended to maintain international peace.

Ans. Members of the League of Nations were expected to resolve disputes through arbitration and diplomacy to maintain peace.

Q.7 "Poland was re-established as an independent nation after more than a century, receiving territories from Germany, Austria-Hungary and Russia, including the Polish Corridor to the sea."
State the significance of the creation of Poland after World War I.

Ans. Poland gained its sovereignty and secured access to the sea *via* the Polish corridor.

Q.8 On 28th June, 1919, the Treaty of Versailles was signed between the Allied Powers and Germany, officially ending the First World War.

State any one impact this treaty had on Germany after 1919.

Ans. It weakened Germany economically due to heavy war reparations.

TYPE - 2   4 Marks

Short Answer Type Questions

Q.1 How did European imperialism contribute to tensions and ultimately lead to the outbreak of World War I?

Ans. European imperialism contributed to tensions and ultimately led to the outbreak of World War I in the following ways

- European nations competed fiercely for colonies in Africa, Asia, and other regions, creating rivalries and mistrust.
- Germany's late entry into the race for colonial expansion challenged Britain and France, increasing international hostility.
- Disputes over territories, such as the Agadir Crisis of 1911, nearly led to war.
- Economic needs for raw materials, markets, and investments drove imperial ambitions.

Q.2 Before World War I, Germany felt 'encircled' by the Triple Entente, which included France, Russia, and Britain. European countries competed intensely for colonies and strengthened their armies and navies. Germany feared that these rivalries and military build-up threatened its security.

Based on the above passage or text, state any four ways in which imperialism and militarism made Germany feel insecure.

Ans. Imperialism and militarism contributed to the sense of insecurity in the following ways

(i) Imperialism created intense economic rivalry among European nations, as Germany demanded 'a place in the Sun' and clashed with Britain and France over colonial territories.

(ii) Competition for colonies led to mistrust, suspicion, and hostility between powers, especially Germany, Britain and France.

(iii) Militarism glorified military power, leading nations like Germany, France and Britain to increase their armies and navies and to develop new weapons.

(iv) Germany's naval expansion under Admiral Tirpit threatened Britain, which viewed naval supremacy as survival issue.

Q.3 Discuss any four actions or policies of Kaiser Williar II that illustrate his significant impact on Europea politics in the early 20th century?

Ans. Four actions or policies of Kaiser William II tha illustrate his significant impact on European politics i the early 20th century were

(i) Kaiser William II openly expressed Germany's desir for global recognition and colonies, stating tha 'Germany too lives under the Sun,' which increase tensions with Britain and France.

(ii) He expanded the German navy under Admira Tirpitz, challenging Britain's naval supremacy an contributing to the naval arms race.

(iii) Under his leadership, Germany adopted a mor aggressive foreign policy, abandoning Bismarck' careful diplomacy, which destabilising Europea alliances.

(iv) His support for Austria-Hungary during crises in th Balkans, such as after the assassination of Archduk Franz Ferdinand, played a key role in the outbreak c World War I.

Q.4 How did nationalism in the Balkans contribute to th outbreak of World War I?

Ans. Nationalism in the Balkans contributed to the outbrea of World War I in the following ways

- Nationalism in the Balkans created strong feeling of pride and a desire for independence amon different ethnic groups.
- Serbia wanted to unite all the Slavic people into on state, but Austria-Hungary opposed this to kee control over Bosnia and Herzegovina.
- Russia supported Serbia as the protector of th Slavic people, which increased tensions wit Austria-Hungary.
- These rivalries and nationalist conflicts eventua led to the assassination of Archduke Frar Ferdinand in 1914, which triggered World War I.

Q.5 **The Balkan Wars (1912–1913) destabilised the region before World War I. Analyse how these events influenced the political tensions in Europe.**

Ans. The events influenced the political tensions in Europe in the following ways

- The Balkan Wars weakened the Ottoman Empire and intensified competition among the Balkan states.
- Serbia emerged as a major supporter of Slavic nationalist movements, angering Austria-Hungary.
- Russia supported Serbia, while Austria-Hungary opposed it, increasing hostility between the two powers.
- The wars showed the instability of the Balkans which made the region a high risk zone that could easily trigger a larger war.

Q.6 **With reference to the excerpt given above, state any four circumstances that led to the harsh treatment of Germany under the Treaty of Versailles.**

TREATY SIGNED; WAR OVER

The Evening World. FINAL

WILSON LEAVES PARIS; SAILS SUNDAY

GERMANS PLEDGED TO ACT IN GOOD FAITH

CITY'S BELLS RING TIDINGS AS PEACE TREATY IS SIGNED; FLEET JOINS IN CELEBRATION

TREATY SEVERE ON GERMANY, SAYS WILSON, BUT IMPOSES NOTHING SHE CANNOT DO

GUNS BOOM, PLANES FILL AIR; FRENCH CROWDS CHEER PEACE

Ans. Four circumstances that led to the harsh treatment of Germany under the Treaty of Versailles are

(i) Germany was held solely responsible for causing World War I under the War Guilt Clause (Article 231), which humiliated the nation.

(ii) Heavy reparations were demanded from Germany, which weakened its economy and led to inflation and unemployment.

(iii) Germany lost important territories, such as Alsace-Lorraine to France and other lands to Belgium, Denmark and Poland, reducing its industrial and strategic strength.

(iv) Germany's military was severely restricted, limiting its defense capability and political influence in Europe. The creation of new states and redrawn borders left many Germans outside Germany, causing resentment.

Q.7 **State any two key features of the Treaty of Versailles, 1919. Mention any two reasons to explain why it was considered unfair and led to future conflicts in Europe.**

Ans. Two key features of the Treaty of Versailles are

(i) The Treaty of Versailles was signed on 28th June, 1919 between the Allied Powers and Germany.

(ii) It officially ended the First World War and imposed harsh political, territorial, military and economic terms on Germany.

Two reasons the treaty was for being considered unfair are

(i) Germany was not allowed to take part in negotiating the treaty and it had to accept harsh terms.

(ii) The treaty punished Germany heavily with damages and territorial losses, which created anger, resentment and a desire for revenge.

Q.8 **State any four reasons to explain why the League of Nations failed to maintain peace in Europe after World War I.**

Ans. The League of Nations failed to maintain peace in Europe after World War I because of the following reasons

(i) The League of Nations lacked enforcement powers and the support of major powers like the USA, making it ineffective.

(ii) Harsh terms of the Treaty of Versailles humiliated Germany and created resentment, leading to instability.

(iii) Many new nations created after the war had mixed populations, leading to minority problems and political tensions.

(iv) The absence of proper negotiation with defeated countries made the League appear unfair and biased.

TYPE - 3 — 8 Marks

Long Answer Type Questions

Q.1 **Discuss any eight features of the Alliance System in Europe before World War I.**

Ans. Eight features of the Alliance System in Europe before World War I are

(i) The alliance system divided Europe into two armed camps which were Triple Alliance and Triple Entente, which made peace weak and unstable.

(ii) Countries believed that forming alliances would protect them, but these alliances increased fear and tension among nations.

(iii) In 1879, Germany and Austria-Hungary signed the Dual Alliance to support each other in case of war. Later, Italy joined Germany and Austria-Hungary and together they formed the Triple Alliance.

(iv) The Triple Alliance followed a defensive policy under Bismarck to maintain peace in Europe.

(v) When Kaiser William II came to power, the alliance became aggressive in nature.

(vi) In response to this, Britain, France and Russia signed a series of agreements between 1894 and 1907. These agreements led to the formation of the Triple Entente.

(vii) As a result, Germany felt surrounded by France and Russia on land and by Britain and France at sea.

(viii) Therefore, the alliance system increased mistrust and ensured that even a small local conflict could turn into a large-scale war.

Q.2 "This war was a result of alliances, militarism and nationalist tensions in Europe."

With reference to the outbreak of World War I, answer the following questions.

(a) State any four long-term causes of World War I.

(b) Explain four short-term causes of the war.

Ans. (a) Four long-term causes of World War I are

(i) The Alliance System divided Europe into two rival groups, the Triple Alliance and the Triple Entente, which increased mistrust and made conflicts likely to spread.

(ii) Militarism led to an arms race and the glorification of military power in European countries.

(iii) Imperialism caused intense rivalry over colonies and trade markets among European powers.

(iv) Nationalism in the Balkans and Europe created tensions, with groups like Serbia seeking unity for Slavs and Germany promoting Pan-Germanism.

(b) The four short-term causes of the war are as follows

(i) **Annexation of Bosnia-Herzegovina (1908)** Austria-Hungary annexed Bosnia-Herzegovina, which angered Serbia and Russia. This increased hostility in the Balkans and intensified rivalry among European powers.

(ii) **Rise of Balkan Nationalism** Nationalist movements grew stronger in the Balkans, especially among Slavs who wanted independence from Austria-Hungary. Serbia emerged as a major supporter of these nationalist aspirations.

(iii) **Formation of Rival Alliances** Europe was divided into two opposing alliance systems- the Triple Alliance and the Triple Entente. These alliances created deep mutual suspicion (mistrust) among European powers. As each group made military plans against the other, even a small conflict was likely to spread quickly and involve many countries.

(iv) **Assassination of Archduke Franz Ferdinand (1914)** The murder of the Austrian heir in Sarajevo by a Serbian nationalist acted as the immediate trigger which led Austria-Hungary to declare war on Serbia.

Q.3 Discuss any eight features of the Paris Peace Settlements (1919–1920).

Ans. Eight features of the Paris Peace Settlements (1919–1920) are

(i) The settlements aimed to reorganise Europe and maintain peace after World War I.

(ii) Austria-Hungary was divided into Austria, Hungary, Czechoslovakia and Yugoslavia.

(iii) The Ottoman Empire lost most of its territories. Turkey survived as an independent state.

(iv) Germany returned Alsace-Lorraine to France and lost other territories to Belgium, Denmark and Poland.

(v) Poland was re-created as an independent nation with access to the sea.

(vi) Finland, Latvia, Lithuania and Estonia emerged as independent states from former Russian territories.

(vii) The new states faced problems because nationalism was not applied equally.

(viii) The settlements created unresolved issues, which later contributed to World War II.

Q.4 On 28th June 1919, the Treaty was signed and officially ended World War I.

(Source: Historical Records)

(a) Identify the Treaty referred to. State any three key clauses of the Treaty.

(b) Discuss any four reasons why the Allied Powers accepted the Treaty despite its flaws.

Ans. (a) The Treaty referred to is the Treaty of Versailles, 1919. The three key clauses of the treaty were

(i) Germany was held solely responsible for causing the first World War I (War Guilt Clause, Article 231).

(ii) Germany was compelled to pay heavy war reparations to the Allied Powers.

(iii) Germany lost territories such as Alsace-Lorraine to France and partition of territory to Belgium, Denmark, and Poland.

(b) Four reasons of why the Allied Powers accepted the Treaty despite its flaws are

(i) The Allied Powers wanted to ensure that Germany would never become strong enough to start another war.

(ii) They sought economic compensation for the massive destruction caused by the war through reparations.

(iii) Redrawing national boundaries and creating new states aimed to satisfy the nationalist aspirations of different ethnic groups in Europe.

(iv) The creation of the League of Nations was seen as a mechanism to maintain long-term peace in Europe.

Q.5 **Discuss the critical evaluation of the Treaty of Versailles.**

Ans. The critical evaluation of the Treaty of Versailles is as follows

- The Treaty of Versailles was meant to create lasting peace after the First World War.
- It punished Germany heavily by making it accept full responsibility for the war through the war guilt clause.
- Germany lost significant territory, colonies and its overseas possessions under the treaty.
- The treaty limited Germany's military strength, allowing only a small army and banning tanks, submarines, and the possession of an airforce.
- Germany was required to pay huge reparations, which created economic hardship and anger among its people.
- The United States did not approve the treaty, which weakened its authority and effectiveness.
- The treaty ignored the principle of self-determination in many regions, leaving minority groups dissatisfied.
- Because of these harsh and unfair terms, the treaty created anger in Germany and contributed to political instability, which later initiated World War II.

8

THE GREAT DEPRESSION

- The Great Depression was a major worldwide economic crisis that began with the Wall Street Crash of 1929 in the United States.
- The crash exposed serious weaknesses in the American economy such as overproduction, unequal distribution of wealth and uncontrolled buying and selling in the stock market.
- The economic crisis soon spread to other countries, especially Germany and Japan, which led to unemployment, industrial decline and political instability.

Causes leading to the Wall Street Crash

- American industries expanded rapidly during the 1920s and produced goods in large quantities, while the purchasing power of people did not increase at the same rate, which resulted in overproduction and declining profits.
- Wealth in the United States was unequally distributed. A small section of society became very rich while the majority of people earned low wages, which limited consumer spending and weakened the economy.
- A large number of people invested in the stock market with the intention of making quick profits rather than long-term investments. This caused share prices to rise far above the actual value of companies.
- Many investors extensively purchased shares on margin by paying only a small amount of their own money and borrowing the rest from banks. This made the stock market extremely unstable and risky.
- Banks played an irresponsible role by giving easy loans and investing depositors' money in the stock market. This made the banking system vulnerable to collapse.
- The government neglected to regulate the stock market and banking system effectively, which allowed speculation, unsafe loans and financial misuse to continue unchecked.
- The agricultural sector was already in crisis after World War I, as farmers faced a fall in crop prices and heavy debts. This reduced rural incomes and affected the overall economy.
- When share prices began to fall in October 1929, panic spread among investors. This led to mass selling of shares and a sudden collapse of the stock market.

Impact on the USA

- The Wall Street Crash led to the closure of thousands of banks in the United States, as people rushed to withdraw their savings and banks were insolvent and unable to return the deposited money.
- Share prices collapsed rapidly and by 1932 the value of stocks had fallen by nearly 80 percent.
- Many industries and business firms suffered heavy losses and were forced to shut down, which resulted in a sharp decline in industrial production.
- Unemployment increased rapidly as factories closed and workers were dismissed, which left 14 million of Americans without jobs or regular income.

Unemployed Americans Standing in Long Queues

REVISION NOTES

- People lost their life savings due to bank failures and falling share prices, resulting in widespread poverty and financial insecurity.
- Farmers suffered heavily as agricultural prices fell due to competition from countries like Canada, Argentina and Australia, and pushed many into poverty.
- International trade of the United States declined sharply because demand for American goods fell both at home and abroad.
- The standard of living of people declined as wages were reduced, prices fell and many families struggled to meet basic needs.

Homeless Children

- The economic crisis led to social problems such as homelessness, hunger and loss of confidence in the American economic system.
- The crash forced the US government to increase its role in the economy, which led to new policies and reforms in later years to control banks and industries.

Impact on Germany

- Germany was heavily dependent on American loans under the Dawes and Young Plans, and when the United States withdrew these loans after the crash, the German economy collapsed rapidly.
- Many German banks and industries faced severe financial crisis and were forced to close, which led to a sharp decline in industrial production.
- Unemployment increased drastically in Germany as factories shut down and workers lost their jobs. This created widespread poverty and hardship and by 1932 more than six million Germans were without jobs.
- The German government faced serious financial difficulties and was unable to provide adequate support to the unemployed or stabilise the economy.
- Farmers and small businessmen suffered heavily due to falling prices, reduced demand and lack of credit facilities.
- The economic crisis weakened the Weimar Republic, as people lost faith in democratic government and its ability to solve their problems.
- Political instability increased as extremist parties gained popularity by promising strong leadership and economic recovery.
- The Nazi Party under Adolf Hitler took advantage of the economic suffering and public dissatisfaction to gain mass support.

Impact of Great Depression; Children demanded job for their Father.

Impact on Japan

- The Wall Street Crash caused a sharp fall in world trade, which badly affected Japan's export-based economy.
- More than forty countries raised tariff barriers to protect their own industries, which severely reduced Japan's exports.
- The American market stopped importing Japanese silk, resulting in the collapse of the silk industry and impacting millions of farmers.
- Many factories in Japan reduced production or closed down, resulting in widespread unemployment and wage cuts. Farmers suffered severely as agricultural prices fell, especially the price of silk, which was a major source of rural income.
- Poverty and economic hardship increased among workers and peasants, creating social unrest in the country.
- The Japanese government faced difficulties in managing the economic crisis and failed to provide effective relief measures. The economic problems weakened democratic institutions and increased dissatisfaction with civilian governments.
- Military leaders gained greater influence by promising economic recovery through territorial expansion and control over resources.
- To overcome economic problems and secure markets and resources, Japan invaded Manchuria in 1931, and later subsequently expanding into China and adopted aggressive and fascist-style policies.

Roosevelt and the New Deal

Franklin D. Roosevelt

- Franklin D. Roosevelt was the President of the United States, he came to power in 1933 during the period of the Great Depression, which followed the Wall Street Crash of 1929.
- To deal with the crisis, President Franklin D. Roosevelt introduced the New Deal, which aimed to provide relief, economic recovery and long-term reforms.
- The main purpose of the New Deal was to provide relief to the unemployed and the poor, promote economic recovery, and reform the financial system to prevent future economic disasters.

Aims of the New Deal

- **Restore Confidence in Banks** The New Deal aimed to rebuild public trust in the banking system, as many people had lost their savings due to bank failures. The government took control of weak banks, closed unsafe banks and allowed only stable banks to function, which encouraged people to deposit money again.
- **Revive Industry and Agriculture** Industries and farms were suffering due to low demand and falling prices. The New Deal introduced government support and regulation to increase production, stabilise markets, and raise farm prices so that industries and farmers could recover financially.
- **Reduce Unemployment** Millions of Americans were unemployed during the Great Depression. The New Deal created jobs through public works programmes such as building roads, dams, bridges and schools, which helped people earn wages and support their families.
- **Improve Purchasing Power** The New Deal aimed to increase the purchasing power of ordinary Americans by raising wages, which improved working conditions and provided employment. When people had more money to spend, demand for goods increased, which helped industries grow.
- **Provide Social Security** The New Deal introduced social security measures to support vulnerable groups such as the widows, the orphans, the elderly and the disabled. These measures provided financial assistance and protection and ensured basic security during times of economic hardship.

Measures Taken by Roosevelt

- **Banking Reforms** All banks in the United States were closed temporarily to check their financial condition. Only those banks that were found to be financially stable were reopened under government supervision and depositors were given guarantees to restore confidence in the banking system.
- **Public Works Administration (PWA)** The Public Works Administration started large construction projects such as building schools, roads, bridges, dams and industries. These projects provided employment to millions of unemployed people and helped improve national infrastructure.
- **National Recovery Administration (NRA)** The National Recovery Administration was set up to end harmful competition among industries. It encouraged firms to cooperate by fixing wages, working hours and prices, and firms that followed these rules were rewarded with the Blue Eagle symbol.
- **Agricultural Reforms** The government introduced agricultural reforms to control overproduction by limiting farm output. Farmers were given subsidies to reduce production, which helped raise agricultural prices and increase farmers' incomes.
- **Tennessee Valley Authority (TVA)** This authority built dams to control floods, provide irrigation and generate cheap electricity. It also introduced improved farming methods, which helped develop one of the poorest regions of the United States.
- **Stock Market Regulation** New laws were passed to control the stock market and prevent reckless speculation. These laws aimed to protect investors, and reduce the possibility of another financial crisis.
- **Social Security Act (1935)** The Social Security Act of 1935 provided pensions to the elderly, unemployment benefits to jobless workers, and financial assistance to widows, orphans, the disabled, and other vulnerable groups.

EXAM ORIENTED QUESTIONS

TYPE - 1   1 Mark

Multiple Choice Questions

Q.1 Identify the key difference between speculation in the share market and long-term investment during the 1920s in the United States.

(a) Speculation involved careful study of company profits, while long-term investment was aimed at quick gains.
(b) Speculation aimed at quick profits, while long-term investment was based on the real value and performance of companies.
(c) Speculation was encouraged by strict government regulation, while long-term investment was uncontrolled.
(d) Speculation reduced risks for investors, while long-term investment increased risks.

Ans. (b) Speculation aimed at quick profits, while long-term investment was based on the real value and performance of companies.

Q.2 Which of the following is considered to be the most serious economic weakness revealed by the Wall Street Crash of 1929?

(a) Excessive government control over industries.
(b) Overdependence on agriculture.
(c) Uncontrolled speculation and weak banking regulation.
(d) Lack of industrial growth.

Ans. (c) Uncontrolled speculation and weak banking regulation.

Q.3 The extract given below refers to the sudden collapse of the Wall Street Stock Exchange in October 1929, which triggered a worldwide economic depression.

Santa Ana Register
FINAL EDITION
BILLIONS LOST AS STOCKS CRASH
Pantages In Jail Awaits Sentence To State Prison
SENATE "FARM BLOC" STARTS BATTLE FOR HIGHER TARIFFS
MAINSTAYS OF MARKET IN PLUNGE

Which of the following factors directly contributed to the collapse of Wall Street?

P : Excessive speculation in the share market
Q : Buying of shares on margin
R : Strict government control over banking
S : Overproduction in industries

(a) P and Q
(b) R and S
(c) P and S
(d) Q and R

Ans. (a) P and Q

Q.4 The image below depicts unemployed Americans standing in long queues outside relief centres during the Great Depression of the 1930s.

Which one of the following best explains the widespread decline of faith in democratic institutions during this period?

(a) The failure of democratic governments to control overproduction in agriculture.
(b) The inability of democratic governments to provide effective economic relief and employment.
(c) The influence of socialist ideologies on working-class movements.
(d) The growing demand for colonial expansion to secure raw materials.

Ans. (b) The inability of democratic governments to provide effective economic relief and employment.

Q.5 Which of the following outcomes of the Great Depression had the greatest impact on the rise of authoritarian regimes in the 1930s?

(a) Decline in international trade.
(b) Rise in agricultural production.
(c) Loss of faith in democratic governments.
(d) Growth of labour unions.

Ans. (c) Loss of faith in democratic governments.

Q.6 Which of the following developments during the Great Depression is considered to be the most significant factor in the rise of Nazism in Germany?
(a) Germany's defeat in the First World War.
(b) Withdrawal of American loans and massive unemployment.
(c) Harsh terms of the Treaty of Versailles alone.
(d) Cultural nationalism promoted by German intellectuals.

Ans. (b) Withdrawal of American loans and massive unemployment.

Q.7 "The economic crisis weakened democratic institutions and increased dissatisfaction with civilian governments. Military leaders gained greater influence by promising economic recovery through territorial expansion and control over resources."

Identify the country being referred to in the above statement.
(a) United States of America
(b) Germany
(c) Japan
(d) Italy

Ans. (c) Japan

Q.8 Who among the following leaders introduced the 'New Deal' to provide relief, recovery and reforms during the Great Depression?
(a) Herbert Hoover (b) Winston Churchill
(c) Franklin D. Roosevelt (d) Harry Truman

Ans. (c) Franklin D. Roosevelt

Q.9 Which of the following actions taken by the United States Government during the Great Depression had goals similar to modern government welfare measures aimed at social security?
(a) Stock market deregulation to encourage private investment.
(b) Introduction of the Social Security Act to support the elderly and unemployed.
(c) Reduction of taxes on wealthy industrialists.
(d) Withdrawal of government control over banks.

Ans. (b) Introduction of the Social Security Act to support the elderly and unemployed.

Q.10 Which of the following New Deal measures is regarded as the most effective in providing immediate relief for the unemployed?
(a) Stock market regulation
(b) Agricultural production control
(c) Public works programmes such as the PWA
(d) Banking reforms

Ans. (c) Public works programmes such as the PWA

Assertion-Reason Questions

Given below are two statements marked as Assertion (A) and Reason (R). Read the two statements carefully and choose the correct answer from the codes given below.

Codes
(a) Both A and R are true and R is the correct explanation of A.
(b) Both A and R are true, but R is not the correct explanation of A.
(c) A is true, but R is false.
(d) Both A and R are false.

Q.1 **Assertion** (A) The Wall Street Crash of 1929 led to widespread unemployment and poverty in the United States.
Reason (R) Many industries closed down after the crash due to falling demand and heavy financial losses.

Ans. (a) Both A and R are true and R is the correct explanation of A.

Q.2 **Assertion** (A) Germany experienced severe political instability during the Great Depression.
Reason (R) The United States withdrew loans from Germany after the Wall Street Crash of 1929, causing banks and industries to collapse.

Ans. (a) Both A and R are true and R is the correct explanation of A.

Q.3 **Assertion** (A) Franklin D. Roosevelt introduced the Social Security Act of 1935.
Reason (R) It provided financial assistance to the elderly, unemployed, widows, orphans and disabled persons during the Great Depression.

Ans. (a) Both A and R are true and R is the correct explanation of A.

Very Short Answer Type Questions

Q.1 "Germany was heavily dependent on American loans under the Dawes and Young Plans, and when the United States withdrew these loans after the crash the German economy collapsed rapidly."
State any one impact this event had on Germany.

Ans. One impact was political instability, as economic hardship weakened the Weimar Republic and led to the rise of extremist parties such as the Nazi party.

Q.2 "The Japanese silk farmers and factory workers suffered due to falling prices and reduced international trade after the Wall Street Crash."
State the impact of this event in Japanese politics.

Ans. The crash of the wall street exchange weakened democratic institutions and increased the influence of military leaders in Japan, which led to territorial expansion in Manchuria and aggressive policies in Asia.

Q.3 The image given below shows unemployed Americans standing in long queues outside a bank during the Great Depression.

State the name of the President who introduced measures to deal with this crisis.

Ans. Franklin D. Roosevelt

Q.4 President Franklin D. Roosevelt introduced the .... to provide relief, economic recovery and long-term reforms during the Great Depression.

Ans. New Deal

Q.5 Expand SSA.

Ans. Social Security Act

Q.6 Mention any one measure of the New Deal that provided financial security to vulnerable groups in the United States.

Ans. The Social Security Act (1935) provided pensions to the elderly, unemployment benefits to jobless workers, and financial assistance to the widows, the orphans and the disabled, improving their economic security during the Great Depression.

TYPE - 2 — 4 Marks

Short Answer Type Questions

Q.1 With reference to the extract showing Americans queuing outside banks and factories shutting down during the Great Depression, state any four factors that worsened the economic situation in the United States in the 1930s.

THE KLAMATH NEWS

"Throw Away Your Hammer—Get Out Your Horn"

STOCKS LOSE 10 BILLION IN DAY

Pantages Convicted; Weeps In Jail With Children

Part Of Attack Enacted For Jury

Bonds On Paving In Mills To Be Sold

Kesterson's Present Logging Operations

Largest Break In History Recorded

Ans. Four circumstances that worsened the economic situation in the United States in the 1930s are as follows

(i) Overproduction in industries led to a situation where factories produced more goods than the people could buy, causing profits to decline and factories to shut down.

(ii) Unequal distribution of wealth meant that a small section of society became extremely wealthy while most people earned low wages, which limited consumer spending and weakened the economy.

(iii) Speculation in the stock market created instability, as many people invested in shares to make quick profits rather than long-term investments, causing share prices to rise far above their real value.

(iv) Bank failures occurred because banks gave easy loans and invested depositors' money in the stock market, which made the banking system extremely vulnerable to a total collapse.

Q.2 The graph given below shows the decline in agricultural prices and farm incomes in the United States during the Great Depression.

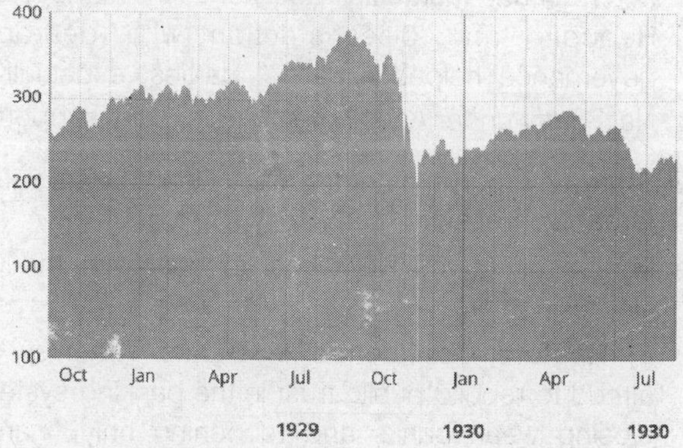

With reference to the above graph, explain the main problems faced by American farmers during the Great Depression.

Ans. The main problems faced by American farmers during the Great Depression are

- **Falling Crop Prices** Farmers received very low prices for their produce due to overproduction and international competition from countries like Canada, Argentina and Australia.
- **Heavy Debts** Many farmers had borrowed money to expand their farms, but declining incomes made it difficult to repay loans.
- **Reduced Rural Incomes** Low prices and debts reduced the purchasing power of farmers, causing widespread poverty in rural areas.
- **Economic Hardship and Social Distress** Farmers struggled to meet basic needs, leading to social instability in farming communities.

Q.3 **"The German banks and industries collapsed after the withdrawal of American loans following the Wall Street Crash of 1929. Millions lost their jobs, and extremist political parties gained popularity."**

Based on the above report, state any four impacts of the Great Depression on Germany.

Ans. Four impacts of the Great Depression on Germany are

(i) **Collapse of Banks and Industries** Many German banks and industrial firms faced severe financial crises and were forced to close, leading to a sharp decline in industrial production.

(ii) **Mass Unemployment** Factories shut down and millions of workers lost their jobs; by 1932, more than six million Germans were unemployed.

(iii) **Economic Hardship for Farmers and Small Businessmen** Falling prices, reduced demand and lack of credit pushed many into poverty.

(iv) **Political Instability** Loss of faith in the Weimar Republic and dissatisfaction with democratic governance helped extremist parties, especially the Nazi Party under Adolf Hitler to gain mass support.

Q.4 **State any four aims of the New Deal to deal with the Great Depression.**

Ans. Four aims of the New Deal to deal with the Great Depression are

(i) **Restore Confidence in Banks** The New Deal aimed to rebuild public trust in the banking system by closing weak banks and reopening only financially sound ones under government supervision.

(ii) **Revive Industry and Agriculture** The New Deal sought to stabilise markets, raise farm prices, and support industries and farmers financially.

(iii) **Reduce Unemployment** Millions of Americans were unemployed during the Great Depression, and the New Deal created jobs through public works programs such as building roads, schools, bridges and dams.

(iv) **Provide Social Security** The New Deal introduced measures to support widows, orphans, the elderly and the disabled, ensuring basic financial protection during economic hardship.

Q.5 **Discuss any four achievements of Franklin D. Roosevelt that justify his New Deal being considered a turning point in the economic recovery of the United States during the Great Depression.**

Ans. Four achievements of Franklin D. Roosevelt that justify his New Deal being considered a turning point in the economic recovery of the United States during the Great Depression are

(i) **Restored Public Trust in Banks** Roosevelt introduced banking reforms, temporarily closing all banks and reopening only financially sound ones under government supervision, which restored public trust in the banking system.

(ii) **Generated Employment through Public Works** The Public Works Administration (PWA) created millions of jobs by building roads, schools, bridges, dams and other infrastructure projects.

(iii) **Improved Social Security** The Social Security Act (1935) provided pensions to the elderly, unemployment benefits to workers and financial assistance to widows, orphans, and the disabled, thereby ensuring social protection.

(iv) **Regulated Industry and Agriculture** Through the National Recovery Administration (NRA) and agricultural reforms, Roosevelt stabilised wages, working hours, prices, and farm incomes, helping industries and farmers recover financially.

Q.6 **State any four important measures taken by the US government to tackle the Great Depression.**

Ans. Four important measures taken by the US government to tackle the Great Depression are

(i) **Banking Reforms** All banks were temporarily closed to check their financial condition. Only financially stable banks were reopened under government supervision and depositors' money was guaranteed to restore confidence.

(ii) **Public Works Administration (PWA)** Large construction projects, such as building schools, roads, bridges, dams and industries, were launched to provide employment and improve national infrastructure.

(iii) **National Recovery Administration (NRA)** The NRA regulated industry by encouraging firms to fix wages, working hours and prices. Firms that followed these rules were rewarded with the 'Blue Eagle' symbol.

(iv) **Tennessee Valley Authority (TVA)** Dams were built to control floods, provide irrigation, generate electricity, and improve farming methods, helping to develop one of the poorest regions in the United States.

TYPE - 3 — 8 Marks

Long Answer Type Questions

Q.1 **The extract shows Americans queuing outside banks and factories shutting down during the Great Depression, leading to widespread poverty and unemployment.**

(a) Identify the set of economic measures introduced by Franklin D. Roosevelt to deal with the crisis. State any three key provisions of these measures.

(b) Discuss any four reasons why the New Deal was considered successful in addressing the problems caused by the Great Depression.

Ans. (a) The set of economic measures New Deal was introduced by Franklin D. Roosevelt.

The three key provisions are

(i) Weak banks were closed, financially sound banks reopened under supervision, and depositors' money was protected.

(ii) Large construction projects were launched to provide employment and improve infrastructure.

(iii) Social Security Act (1935) provided pensions, unemployment benefits and financial assistance to vulnerable groups.

(b) The New Deal was considered successful in addressing the problems caused by the Great Depression because

(i) **Restored Public Confidence** Banking reforms and stock market regulations stabilised financial institutions.

(ii) **Reduced Unemployment** PWA projects and other public works created millions of jobs.

(iii) **Improved Social Welfare** The Social Security Act provided economic security for the elderly, disabled, widows and orphans.

(iv) **Revived Industries and Agriculture** NRA and agricultural reforms helped stabilise prices, wages and production, aiding economic recovery.

Q.2 **"The decline in Japanese exports and the collapse of the silk industry created widespread poverty and social unrest in Japan during the early 1930s."**

With reference to Japan during the Great Depression, answer the following questions.

(a) State any four causes that worsened the economic situation in Japan.

(b) Discuss any two reasons each for the rise of military influence in Japan and the social unrest among workers and peasants.

Ans. (a) Four causes of economic worsening in Japan are

(i) **Fall in World Trade** The Wall Street Crash caused a sharp decline in global trade, reducing demand for Japanese exports.

(ii) **High Tariffs Abroad** Over forty countries raised tariff barriers to protect their own industries, severely restricting Japanese exports.

(iii) **Collapse of the Silk Industry** The American market stopped importing Japanese silk, which was a major source of rural income.

(iv) **Factory Closures and Unemployment** Many factories reduced production or shut down, resulting in wage cuts and job losses.

(b) Two reasons for the rise of military influence are

(i) Economic hardships weakened civilian governments, giving military leaders the opportunity to promise recovery through territorial expansion.

(ii) The military exploited nationalist sentiment and the need for resources to gain political power.

Two reasons for social unrest among workers and peasants were

(i) Widespread unemployment and wage cuts led to poverty and discontent among industrial workers.

(ii) Falling agricultural prices, especially in the silk industry, caused severe hardship for farmers, sparking protests and social unrest.

Q.3 Discuss the impact of the New Deal on the democratic and economic system in the United States.

Ans. The impact of the New Deal on the democratic and economic system in the United States are

- The New Deal strengthened the federal government's role in the economy, as it took active measures to regulate banks, industries and agriculture.
- Banking reforms under the New Deal restored public confidence in the financial system, preventing further panic and collapse.
- The stock market was regulated, reducing reckless speculation and protecting investors, which stabilised the economy.
- Public Works Administration (PWA) projects created millions of jobs, providing wages and reducing unemployment.
- The New Deal improved purchasing power of ordinary Americans, which increased demand for goods and supported economic recovery.
- Social Security Act (1935) provided pensions, unemployment benefits, and assistance to widows, orphans and the disabled, ensuring social security.
- By addressing economic hardship, the New Deal reduced social unrest and strengthened people's faith in democratic institutions.
- Overall, the New Deal introduced long-term reforms that shaped the US democratic and economic system to respond to citizens' needs effectively.

RISE OF COMMUNISM UNDER STALIN IN RUSSIA (1917-1939)

The Russian Revolution of 1917

- The Russian Revolution of 1917 overthrew the monarchy and led to the establishment of a communist government under the Bolsheviks.
- Under the leadership of Lenin, the Soviet Union adopted policies like the New Economic Policy to rebuild the economy and stabilise the country after the Civil War.
- After Lenin's death in 1924, Joseph Stalin gradually emerged as the leader of the Soviet Union by consolidating power within the Communist Party.
- Stalin's rule was marked by rapid industrialisation, collectivisation of agriculture, and strict political control through purges and propaganda.

Russian Revolution

Causes of the March Revolution

- The March Revolution was caused by the autocratic rule of Tsar Nicholas II, who followed a monarchical system and denied the people political rights, leading to widespread public dissatisfaction.
- Russia's entry into the First World War placed a heavy economic burden on the country, which increased public unrest and contributed directly to the March Revolution.
- The failure of industries during the war led to acute shortages of food, fuel, and essential goods, causing sharp rises in prices and severe hardship for workers and the poor.
- Industrial workers were forced to work long hours in unhealthy conditions for very low wages, which intensified resentment against the Tsarist government.
- Heavy military losses and a meaningless war effort demoralised soldiers, making them unwilling to support the Tsar's regime.
- Food shortages led to mass protests by workers in Petrograd, and when soldiers refused to suppress these protests, the movement strengthened and resulted in the March Revolution.

Tsar Nicholas II

Results of the March Revolution

- The March Revolution spread across Russia, and Tsar Nicholas II lost the support of both the army and the people. Therefore, he was forced to abdicate (vacate) the throne, which ended the Romanov dynasty.
- After the fall of the monarchy, a provisional government was formed under Lvov and later Kerensky.
- With the establishment of the provisional government, Russia was declared a republic and the new government conferred civil liberties such as freedom of speech, press, and assembly.
- At the same time, Soviets, which were councils of workers and soldiers, emerged as powerful political bodies.
- As a result, a system of dual power developed in Russia in which both the provisional government and the Soviets claimed authority.

Weaknesses of the Provisional Government Leading to the November Revolution

- The provisional government decided to continue fighting in World War I. This caused huge losses, food shortages, and economic collapse. Soldiers and civilians became angry and lost trust in the government.
- Peasants wanted immediate redistribution of land from landlords. The government delayed land reforms, stating that these would be decided later by the Constituent Assembly, which frustrated peasants.
- Inflation rose sharply, industries collapsed, and unemployment increased. Workers suffered from low wages and food shortages, leading to strikes and unrest.
- The provisional government shared power with the 'Petrograd Soviet' system of Dual Power. This made decision-making ineffective and confusing, and the government could not enforce its policies properly.
- The government mainly represented middle-class and elite interests. Workers, soldiers, and peasants felt ignored and turned toward the Bolsheviks.
- The soldiers were tired of the war and discipline broke down. Many soldiers shifted their support to the Soviets and subsequently the Bolsheviks withdrawing their allegiance from the government.
- Elections to the Constituent Assembly were repeatedly postponed. People felt the government was not truly democratic.
- Because of these weaknesses, the provisional government lost credibility and support. The Bolsheviks, under Lenin, promised 'Peace, Land and Bread', which appealed to the masses and led to the November Revolution of 1917.

Lenin

Reasons for the New Economic Policy (NEP)

Lenin

- Lenin initially introduced War Communism during the Civil War, which nationalised all industries and seized grain. This created unrest and economic breakdown.
- To stabilise the country, Lenin introduced the New Economic Policy (NEP) in 1921.
- His aim was to revive production, reduce dissatisfaction, and balance socialism with limited private enterprises.

Impact of the New Economic Policy (NEP)

- The New Economic Policy helped to stimulate agriculture by allowing peasants to sell their surplus produce in the market, which increased food availability.
- Small private businesses and trade were permitted, which improved the supply of goods and living conditions in towns and cities.
- Industrial production gradually recovered as some private enterprises were allowed to operate.
- The policy reduced unrest among peasants and workers and brought stability to the economy.
- However, the NEP also led to the emergence of a new class of wealthier peasants called 'kulaks' and created some economic inequality in society.

Rise of Stalin to Power

Stalin

- Lenin died in 1924 and his death triggered a struggle for leadership in the Communist Party because no clear successor was appointed.
- The main opponents were Joseph Stalin, who was the General Secretary of the party, and Leon Trotsky, who was a popular and influential leader.
- Stalin used his position as General Secretary to appoint his supporters to key positions within the party and gradually, he gained control over the party.
- He promoted the idea of 'Socialism in One Country', which appealed to party members, while Trotsky wanted to focus on spreading revolution internationally.
- Stalin strategically formed alliances with other party leaders to isolate Trotsky and weaken his influence.

- Through propaganda, Stalin presented himself as the true follower of Lenin's ideas and portrayed Trotsky as a threat to the party.
- By 1927, Trotsky was removed from the Communist Party, and in 1929 he was exiled from the Soviet Union and Stalin emerged as the supreme leader of the Soviet Union and consolidated his power.

Factors Assisting Stalin's Rise

- Stalin's position as General Secretary allowed him to control party appointments and build a strong base of loyal supporters.
- Stalin's political skills enabled him to form alliances and manipulate rivalries within the party.
- His ideas, especially 'Socialism in One Country', h were popular among party members and helped him gain support.
- The use of propaganda portrayed him as Lenin's rightful successor, which increased his influence among party members and the public.

Main Features of Stalin's Domestic Policy

Collectivisation of Agriculture

- Stalin introduced collectivisation in the late 1920s to bring all agricultural land under state control and to increase grain production for the growing industrial workforce.
- Individual small farms were merged into large collective farms called kolkhozes and state-run farms called sovkhozes.
- The policy aimed to ensure a stable supply of food for cities and to provide grain for export to generate funds for industrialisation.
- Many peasants, particularly wealthier farmers known as kukas, resisted the collectivisation of agriculture. They were termed as enemies of the state and thousands were executed, imprisoned or deported to remote regions.
- Collectivisation resulted in widespread disruption in agriculture, which caused famine in some areas, especially in Ukraine; however, it also allowed the state to control food distribution and support industrial growth.

Industrialisation: First and Second Five-Year Plans

- Stalin's industrialisation policy aimed to transform the Soviet Union from a backward agrarian country into a modern industrial power.
- **The First Five-Year Plan (1928-1932)** Focused on the development of heavy industries such as steel, coal, iron and machinery. It emphasised state-owned factories and large-scale production.
- **The Second Five-Year Plan (1933-1937)** Built upon the First Five-Year Plan and aimed to further expand industries while improving transport systems, power supply, and communication networks.
- Industrialisation achieved remarkable growth in production, modernised the economy and strengthened the military-industrial base of the USSR.
- However, it also caused harsh working conditions, long hours, strict targets and shortages of consumer goods, which led to widespread hardship amongst workers.

Purges of 1937-1938

- The Purges of 1937-1938 were a series of violent actions carried out by Joseph Stalin to strengthen his power in the Soviet Union. During this period individuals perceived as enemies or threats to Stalin suffered severe punishment.
  - Stalin carried out purges to remove real or suspected enemies from the Communist Party, the Red Army and society.
  - Many party members, Army officers, intellectuals, and ordinary people were arrested, killed or deported to forced-labour camps, collectively known as Gulags.
  - Stalin said the purges were important to protect the revolution, but in reality purges created fear and mistrust among the people.
  - The purges helped Stalin to eliminate his rivals thereby solidifying his authority over the party and on the government very strong.

EXAM ORIENTED QUESTIONS

TYPE - 1 — 1 Mark

Multiple Choice Questions

Q.1 "Industries failed to meet civilian needs and there was an acute shortage of food, fuel, and essential goods."

This situation arose mainly due to Russia's involvement in

(a) the Crimean War
(b) the Russo-Japanese War
(c) the First World War
(d) the Civil War

Ans. (c) the First World War

Q.2 The picture below is of Tsar Nicholas II, the last ruler of the Romanov dynasty in Russia.

Which one of the following best describes the reason for the downfall of Tsar Nicholas II in 1917?

(a) His support for liberal reforms and democracy.
(b) Autocratic rule and failure to address economic and social problems.
(c) His success in leading Russia during the First World War.
(d) Strong cooperation between the Tsar and the Soviets.

Ans. (b) Autocratic rule and failure to address economic and social problems.

Q.3 "The soldiers were ordered by the Tsar to suppress the protests, but they refused to do so. The refusal of soldiers to obey orders directly resulted in:

(a) the formation of Soviets
(b) the March Revolution
(c) the Civil War
(d) the New Economic Policy

Ans. (b) the March Revolution

Q.4 "After the fall of the monarchy, a provisional government was formed under Lvov and later Kerensky."Which major political change followed the formation of the Provisional Government?

(a) Establishment of a communist state.
(b) Introduction of dictatorship.
(c) Declaration of Russia as a republic.
(d) End of the First World War.

Ans. (c) Declaration of Russia as a republic.

Q.5 The extract given above refers to the failure of the provisional government in Russia after the March Revolution of 1917. Which of the following reasons contributed to the loss of public support for the Provisional Government? *Source: Historical Records*

THE PROVISIONAL GOVERNMENT LEADING TO THE NOVEMBER REVOLUTION

The Provisional Government came to power after the March Revolution, but it failed to end Russia's participation in the First World War, which disappointed the people.
As the war continued, economic conditions worsened, and problems such as inflation. unemployment, and food shortages became mor severe.
At the same-time, the government did not introduce land reforms, even though peasants had been demanding land for a long time.
Instead of taking quick action, the Provisional Government delayed important reforms and postponed elections and because of these failures, workers, peasants, and soldiers gradually lost faith in the Provisional Government.

P. Continued participation in the First World War
Q. Delay in land reforms for peasants
R. Immediate improvement in economic conditions
S. Postponement of elections and reforms

(a) P and Q
(b) R and S
(c) P, Q and S
(d) Q and R

Ans. (c) P, Q and S

Q.6 Identify the key difference between the March Revolution and the November Revolution in Russia.

(a) The March Revolution was led by the Bolsheviks, while the November Revolution was spontaneous.
(b) The March Revolution overthrew the monarchy, while the November Revolution overthrew the provisiona government.
(c) The March Revolution established a communis government, while the November Revolution restored the monarchy.
(d) The March Revolution occurred after the Civil War, while the November Revolution occurred before it.

Ans. (b) The March Revolution overthrew the monarchy, while the November Revolution overthrew the provisional government.

Q.7 Who among the following leaders led the Bolsheviks during the Russian Revolution of 1917?
(a) Tsar Nicholas II
(b) Joseph Stalin
(c) Vladimir Lenin
(d) Leon Trotsky

Ans. (c) Vladimir Lenin

Q.8 Identify the key difference between War Communism and the New Economic Policy.
(a) War Communism encouraged private trade, while the NEP abolished it.
(b) War Communism was introduced after 1924, while the NEP was introduced before 1917.
(c) War Communism involved complete state control, while the NEP allowed limited private enterprise.
(d) War Communism focused on agriculture, while the NEP focused only on industry.

Ans. (c) War Communism involved complete state control, while the NEP allowed limited private enterprise.

Q.9 Identify the key difference between Lenin's and Stalin's economic policies.
(a) Lenin promoted complete collectivisation, while Stalin supported private farming.
(b) Lenin followed the NEP with limited capitalism, while Stalin ended it and introduced collectivisation and Five-Year Plans.
(c) Lenin focused only on heavy industry, while Stalin ignored industrial growth.
(d) Lenin ruled after Stalin and reversed his policies.

Ans. (b) Lenin followed the NEP with limited capitalism, while Stalin ended it and introduced collectivisation and Five-Year Plans.

Q.10 Identify the key difference between kolkhozes and sovkhozes.
(a) Kolkhozes were state-owned farms, while sovkhozes were privately owned.
(b) Kolkhozes were collective farms, while sovkhozes were state-run farms.
(c) Kolkhozes existed under the NEP, while sovkhozes existed under War Communism.
(d) Kolkhozes were found in cities, while sovkhozes were found in industrial areas.

Ans. (b) Kolkhozes were collective farms, while sovkhozes were state-run farms.

Assertion-Reason Questions

Given below are two statements marked as Assertion (A) and Reason (R). Read the two statements carefully and choose the correct answer from the codes given below.

Codes
(a) Both A and R are true and R is the correct explanation of A.
(b) Both A and R are true, but R is not the correct explanation of A.
(c) A is true, but R is false.
(d) Both A and R are false.

Q.1 **Assertion** (A) The March Revolution of 1917 led to the end of the Romanov dynasty in Russia.

Reason (R) Tsar Nicholas I lost the support of the army and the people during the revolution.

Ans. (c) A is true, but R is false.

Q.2 **Assertion** (A) A system of dual power developed in Russia after the March Revolution.

Reason (R) Both the Provisional Government and the Soviets claimed authority at the same time.

Ans. (a) Both A and R are true and R is the correct explanation of A.

Q.3 **Assertion** (A) Lenin introduced the New Economic Policy (NEP) in 1921.

Reason (R) War Communism had caused economic breakdown and unrest among peasants and workers.

Ans. (a) Both A and R are true and R is the correct explanation of A.

Q.4 **Assertion** (A) Stalin was able to emerge as the supreme leader of the Soviet Union after Lenin's death.

Reason (R) Stalin used his position as General Secretary to place loyal supporters in key party positions.

Ans. (a) Both A and R are true and R is the correct explanation of A.

Q.5 **Assertion** The purges of 1937-1938 helped Stalin consolidate his power in the Soviet Union.

Reason The purges eliminated real or suspected opponents from the party, army and society.

Ans. (a) Both A and R are true and R is the correct explanation of A.

Very Short Answer Type Questions

Q.1 The Russian Revolution of 1917 led to the establishment of a .... government in Russia.

Ans. Communist

Q.2 In November 1917, the Bolsheviks overthrew the provisional government under the leadership of Lenin. *Source: Russian Revolution records*

State any one impact of this event on the governance of Russia.

Ans. The overthrow of the Provisional Government led to the establishment of a Bolshevik (Communist) regime, marking the beginning of one-party rule under Lenin in Russia.

Q.3 The slogan 'Peace, Bread and Land' was associated with which group during the Russian Revolution of 1917?

Ans. The Bolsheviks.

Q.4 The image given below shows a leader addressing workers and soldiers during the Russian Revolution. *Source: Socialist workers*

Name the leader who headed the Bolsheviks during the November Revolution of 1917.

Ans. Vladimir Lenin

Q.5 Mention any one provision of War Communism during the Russian Civil War.

Ans. All major industries were nationalised and brought under state control.

Q.6 Expand NEP.

Ans. New Economic Policy

Q.7 The New Economic Policy allowed peasants to sell their .... produce in the market.

Ans. Surplus

Q.8 Lenin introduced the New Economic Policy to revive the Soviet economy after the Civil War.

Source: Soviet economic policies

State any one impact of the NEP on the Soviet economy.

Ans. It helped revive agricultural and industrial production by allowing limited private enterprise.

Q.9 The picture shown below features Joseph Stalin whose policies of .... transformed the Soviet Union into a major industrial power.

Ans. Industrialisation and collectivisation

Q.10 The state-run farms introduced under collectivisation were known as ....

Ans. Sovkhozes

Q.11 Mention any one provision of Stalin's policy of collectivisation of agriculture.

Ans. Individual peasant farms were merged into large collective farms called Kolkhozes.

Q.12 The labour camps where political prisoners were sent during Stalin's rule were called ....

Ans. Gulags

Q.13 During 1937-1938, Joseph Stalin carried out large-scale purges in the Soviet Union in which party members, Red Army officers, intellectuals and ordinary citizens were arrested, executed or sent to labour camps (Gulags).

What was the significance of this event in the Soviet Union under Stalin?

Ans. The purges eliminated real and suspected opponents and created an atmosphere of fear and obedience.

TYPE - 2   4 Marks

Short Answer Type Questions

Q.1 With reference to the news extract given below,state any four causes that led to the outbreak of the March Revolution in Russia.

New York Tribune

FRIDAY, MARCH 16, 1917

road Strike Called, Men Quit To-morrow

Strike Chiefs Give New York 5 Days To Get Food Supply

Threaten to Kill Americans Who Fire on U-Boats

Czar of Russia Abandons Throne; Army Revolts and Joins People

FORMER CZAR AND CZARINA OF RUSSIA

Duma Leaders in Complete Control After Fierce Battles; Protopopoff Reported Killed

New Cabinet Is Formed; Prince Lvoff Now Premier

Ans. Four causes that led to the outbreak of the March Revolution in Russia are as follows

(i) Russia was ruled by Tsar Nicholas II, who followed an autocratic system of government and did not give political rights to the people, which created widespread dissatisfaction.

(ii) Russia's participation in the First World War placed a heavy burden on the economy and led to shortages of food, fuel, and essential goods.

(iii) Food prices rose sharply due to shortages, making life extremely difficult for workers and poor people.

(iv) Soldiers suffered heavy losses during the war and refused to suppress protests, which strengthened the workers movement and led to the March Revolution.

Q.2 Discuss any four achievements of Vladimir Lenin that justify his leadership of Soviet Russia after the 1917 Revolution.

Ans. Four achievements of Vladimir Lenin as a leader of Soviet Russia after the 1917 Revolution are as follows

(i) Lenin led the Bolsheviks to overthrow the Provisional Government in the November Revolution of 1917, establishing a communist government in Russia.

(ii) He introduced **War Communism** during the Civil War, which helped the Bolsheviks maintain control and manage the economy under difficult conditions.

(iii) To stabilise the economy, Lenin introduced the New Economic Policy (NEP) in 1921, which revived agriculture, allowed small private businesses, and improved the supply of food and goods.

(iv) Lenin established a strong centralised government and the Soviet system of councils (Soviets), which became the foundation of the Communist Party's rule in Russia.

Q.3 After the March Revolution of 1917, the Provisional Government came to power in Russia. However, workers, peasants, and soldiers were dissatisfied with its performance and unrest continued in the country.

Source: Rise of Communism under Stalin

Based on the above report, state any four reasons for the growing dissatisfaction against the Provisional Government.

Ans. Four reasons for the growing dissatisfaction against the provisional government are given below

(i) The Provisional Government continued Russia's participation in the First World War, which caused heavy losses and disappointment among soldiers.

(ii) Economic conditions worsened, with inflation, unemployment and food shortages becoming more severe.

(iii) The government failed to introduce land reforms, even though peasants had been demanding land for a long time.

(iv) Important reforms were delayed, elections were postponed, and the government appeared weak, causing workers, peasants and soldiers to lose faith in the government's ability to rule.

Q.4 How did the weaknesses of the Provisional Government contribute to its failure and the success of the Bolsheviks in 1917?

Ans. The weaknesses of the Provisional Government contribute to its failure and the success of the Bolsheviks in 1917 can be understood by the following

(i) The provisional government continued Russia's participation in the First World War, causing heavy losses and dissatisfaction among soldiers.

(ii) Economic problems like rising inflation, unemployment, and food shortages made life difficult for workers and peasants.

(iii) The government failed to introduce land reforms and delayed important reforms, losing support among peasants and workers.

(iv) Its weak authority and inability to control the army allowed the Bolsheviks, who promised peace, land, and bread, to gain popular support and overthrow it.

Q.5 Joseph Stalin introduced major changes in the Soviet Union after consolidating power in the Communist Party. His policies included collectivisation of agriculture, rapid industrialisation and political purges to strengthen state control.

In the above context, analyse the impact of Stalin's domestic policies on the Soviet Union.

Ans. The impact of Stalin's domestic policies on the Soviet Union are as follows

- Collectivisation brought agriculture under state control and ensured food supply for cities, but it caused severe hardship, resistance by peasants, and widespread famine in some regions.
- Industrialisation through the Five-Year Plans transformed the Soviet Union into a major industrial power and strengthened its military capacity.
- The focus on heavy industries led to the neglect of consumer goods, resulting in shortages and poor living conditions for workers.
- The purges of 1937-1938 created fear and insecurity in society and eliminated political opposition, strengthening Stalin's dictatorship.

TYPE - 3 8 Marks

Long Answer Type Questions

Q.1 "War Communism created unrest and the economy was in crisis." *Source: Lenin's policy, 1918-1921*

(a) State any four reasons for the introduction of the New Economic Policy (NEP).

(b) Discuss any two positive and two negative effects of the NEP on Soviet society.

Ans. (a) Four reasons for the introduction of the New Economic Policy (NEP) are as follows

(i) War Communism caused a breakdown of the economy and led to widespread dissatisfaction among the people.

(ii) Agricultural production suffered because peasants were forced to give up their grain to the state.

(iii) Many industries collapsed due to nationalisation and poor management, reducing overall production.

(iv) Unrest among workers and peasants increased, threatening the stability and control of the Bolshevik government.

(b) Two positive effects of the NEP on Soviet society are as follows

(i) Agriculture revived because peasants were allowed to sell their surplus produce in the market, which increased food availability.

(ii) Small private businesses and trade were permitted, improving the supply of goods and the living conditions of people in towns and cities.

Two negative effects of the NEP on Soviet society are as follows

(i) The NEP led to the emergence of a new class of wealthier peasants called kulaks, which created some economic inequality in society.

(ii) Some socialists criticised the NEP as a compromise of true socialist principles, believing that it had moved away from full communism.

Q.2 On 21st January 1924, after the death of Lenin, a struggle for leadership began in the Communist Party of the Soviet Union.

Source: Rise of Communism under Stalin

(a) Identify the leader who eventually emerged as the supreme leader of the Soviet Union. State any three methods he used to consolidate his power.

(b) Discuss any four factors that assisted him in gaining support and eliminating his rivals.

Ans. (a) The leader who emerged as the supreme leader of the Soviet Union was Joseph Stalin.

Three methods Stalin used to consolidate power were as follows

(i) Stalin used his position as General Secretary to appoint loyal supporters to key positions in the Communist Party, strengthening his influence.

(ii) He promoted the idea of 'Socialism in One Country' to gain widespread support within the party.

(iii) Stalin used propaganda to present himself as Lenin's true follower thereby portraying his rivals, Trotsky, as threats.

(b) Four factors that assisted Stalin in gaining support and eliminating his rivals were as follows

- **Control Over Party Organisation** As General Secretary, Stalin controlled party appointments and placed his supporters in important positions.
- **Alliance and Isolation Strategy** Stalin first formed alliances with some leaders and then gradually isolated and removed them one by one.

- **Removal of Trotsky** He discredited Trotsky and eventually expelled him from the party and later from the Soviet Union.
- **Use of Secret Police** Stalin used the secret police to suppress opposition and create fear among rivals.

Q.3 **"All agricultural land must be collectivised to support industrial growth."**

Source: Stalin's domestic policy, late 1920s

(a) State any four objectives of collectivisation in the Soviet Union.

(b) Discuss any two positive and two negative consequences of collectivisation.

Ans. (a) Four objectives of collectivisation are as follows

(i) Collectivisation aimed at bringing all agricultural land under state control.

(ii) It sought to increase grain production to feed the growing urban workforce.

(iii) The policy aimed to generate funds for industrialisation through the export of grain.

(iv) Collectivisation also aimed to eliminate the Kulaks, who were wealthy peasants, as a class.

(b) Two positive consequences of collectivisation are as follows

(i) Collectivisation allowed the state to control the food supply, ensuring that the industrial workforce in the cities was adequately fed.

(ii) Grain exports generated funds, which helped finance the rapid industrial growth of the Soviet Union.

Two negative consequences of collectivisation are as follows

(i) Collectivisation caused widespread famine, especially in regions like Ukraine, leading to the death of many peasants.

(ii) Many peasants resisted the policy, and thousands were executed, imprisoned or deported to remote areas.

Q.4 **Discuss any eight features of Stalin's Purges of 1937-1938 in the Soviet Union.**

Ans. Eight features of Stalin's Purges of 1937-1938 in the Soviet Union are as follows

(i) The purges targeted people who were considered enemies of the state.

(ii) Many party members suspected of disloyalty were arrested, imprisoned or executed.

(iii) High-ranking army officers were removed, which weakened potential opposition within the military.

(iv) Intellectuals and ordinary citizens were also targeted during the purges.

(v) Thousands of people were sent to labour camps known as Gulags.

(vi) The purges created a climate of fear and mistrust throughout Soviet society.

(vii) They strengthened Stalin's control over both the Communist Party and the government.

(viii) Although the purges consolidated Stalin's power, they caused the loss of experienced leaders, thereby weakening key institutions in the country.

10

RISE OF FASCISM

Post-War Discontent and the Rise of Benito Mussolini

- After World War I, Italy faced economic problems, high unemployment and social unrest.
- Many Italians were unhappy with the government and felt that Italy had received a 'mutilated victory' this meant that although Italy won World War I, it did not receive all the territories it had been promised. So the victory felt incomplete and disappointing to the Italians.
- In this situation, Benito Mussolini rose to power by promising strong leadership, order, and national pride, eventually becoming Prime Minister in 1922.

Benito Mussolini

Conditions Responsible for the Rise of Fascism in Italy

Economic Problems

- Italy faced severe economic difficulties after World War I, including high unemployment, inflation, and massive war debts, which caused widespread hardship among the population.
- Soldiers who were returning from the war, found few job opportunities, which led to frustration and unrest.

Political Instability

- Italy's parliamentary system was weak which made it incapable of addressing economic and social crises.
- Many Italians lost faith in liberal democracy, believing it was unable to restore order or national pride.

Social Unrest

- Workers and peasants organised strikes, protests and land seizures which were inspired by socialist and communist movements.
- The middle class, industrialists, and landowners feared a socialist revolution, which pushed them to support strong authoritarian leadership.

Nationalist Discontent

- Many Italians were unhappy with the Treaty of London (1915) because Italy did not receive all the territories that had been promised after the war, so they felt their victory was incomplete and unfair.
- Nationalists demanded a stronger Italy that could assert itself on the European stage and restore national pride.

Weakness of the Liberal Government

- The liberal governments failed to manage economic hardships, social conflicts and political instability.
- Their inability to maintain law and order created a power vacuum that extremist movements, like Fascism, could exploit.

Appeal of Strong Leadership

- People desired a leader who could bring stability, discipline, and national revival after the chaos of war and political failure.
- Benito Mussolini promised strong leadership, action against socialists and the revival of Italy's glory, which attracted broad support from different sections of society.

Mussolini's Rise to Power

Fascist Militias in Blackshirts

- In the parliamentary elections of 1921, Mussolini's Fascist Party contested for the first time and won 35 seats and established itself as a recognised political force in Italy.
- Between 1921 and 1922, Mussolini organised Fascist militias called Blackshirts, who attacked socialists, trade unionists and political opponents to threaten them and gain influence.
- The political crisis in 1922, worsened as weak coalition governments failed to address economic difficulties, social unrest and strikes. This created widespread disorder in the country.
- During this period, the Fascists strengthened their influence in local governments and rural areas by using propaganda and nationalist slogans to attract broader support.
- Many Italians began to see Mussolini as a strong leader who could restore law, order and national pride after the chaos of post-war Italy.
- In October 1922, Mussolini and approximately 30,000 Blackshirts threatened to seize power by Marching on Rome. This created a situation of extreme political tension.
- King Victor Emmanuel III refused to declare martial law because of the fear of civil war and invited Mussolini to form a government.
- On 31st October, 1922, Mussolini was appointed Prime Minister of Italy, marking the beginning of Fascist rule in the country.

Main Features of Mussolini's Domestic Policy

Secret Police : OVRA

- Mussolini established a dictatorship by concentrating all power in his own hands and weakening the role of Parliament.
- All political opposition parties were banned and strict censorship was imposed on the press to control public opinion.
- The secret police called OVRA (Organisation for Vigilance and Repression of Anti-Fascism) was created to suppress dissent and punish critics of the Fascist regime.
- Mussolini followed a policy of corporatism, in which workers and employers were organised into state-controlled corporations to prevent class conflict.
- The fascist government launched large public works programmes, such as road building and land reclamation, to reduce unemployment.
- Mussolini aimed at economic self-sufficiency (Autarky) by promoting domestic industries and agriculture.
- Education and youth organisations were used to spread Fascist ideology and promote loyalty to the state and Mussolini.
- Women were encouraged to focus on motherhood and family life in order to increase the population.
- Mussolini signed the Lateran Treaty (1929) with the Pope, improving relations between the Fascist state and the Catholic Church.
- Strong propaganda was used to glorify the state and present Mussolini as a powerful and heroic leader.

Critical Appraisal of Mussolini's Policies

- Mussolini's economic policies helped reduce unemployment in the short term through public works programmes such as road construction and land reclamation projects.
- The policy of corporatism aimed to reduce conflict between workers and employers, however in practice, it favoured employers and limited workers' rights.
- Mussolini's policy of autarky aimed at making Italy economically self-sufficient, but it proved costly and inefficient, as Italy lacked many essential raw materials.
- Agricultural campaigns like the Battle for Grain increased wheat production but it reduced the cultivation of other important crops, thereby disrupting the agricultural equilibrium.
- Industrial growth under Fascism was uneven and primarily benefitted large industries and wealthy industrialists rather than ordinary workers.
- Workers' wages were kept low and trade unions were controlled by the state, leading to poor living standards for the working class.
- Although Mussolini created an image of economic stability through propaganda yet Italy remained economically weak and dependent on imports.
- Politically, Mussolini's authoritarian policies which suppressed opposition and created a police state, thereby limiting freedom of speech and political participation.

EXAM ORIENTED QUESTIONS

TYPE - 1

1 Mark

Multiple Choice Questions

Q.1 Which of the following conditions most strongly contributed to the rise of Fascist ideology in Italy after World War I?

(a) Strong parliamentary democracy and stable governments

(b) Economic hardship, political instability and fear of socialism

(c) Rapid industrial growth and rising living standards

(d) Successful territorial expansion after the war

Ans. (b) Economic hardship, political instability and fear of socialism

Q.2 Which of the following best explains why the middle class and industrialists supported Fascism in Italy after World War I?

(a) Fascism promised expansion of parliamentary democracy.

(b) Fascism protected workers' rights through independent trade unions.

(c) Fascism opposed socialism and promised law, order and stability.

(d) Fascism supported equal distribution of wealth among all classes.

Ans. (c) Fascism opposed socialism and promised law, order and stability.

Q.3 Why did the idea of a 'mutilated victory' help the growth of Fascist ideology in Italy after World War I?

(a) It increased trust in the liberal government and democracy.

(b) It made Italians satisfied with the post-war peace settlement.

(c) It created nationalist resentment and a desire for strong leadership.

(d) It encouraged cooperation with socialist and communist groups.

Ans. (c) It created nationalist resentment and a desire for strong leadership.

Q.4 "In October 1922, Mussolini and his followers threatened to seize power by marching on Rome, which resulted in of extreme political tension in Italy."

What was the immediate result of this event?

(a) The declaration of martial law by the King.

(b) The formation of a socialist government.

(c) Mussolini being invited to form the government.

(d) The fall of the Fascist Party.

Ans. (c) Mussolini being invited to form the government.

Q.5 The following is a picture of Fascist militias known as the Blackshirts, who played a key role in Mussolini's rise to power.

Source: www.britannica.com

Which one of the following best explains how the Blackshirts helped Mussolini become Prime Minister of Italy?

(a) They promoted democratic reforms through peaceful protests.

(b) They used violence and intimidation against political opponents to create fear and instability.

(c) They focused mainly on economic reforms and welfare activities.

(d) They opposed Mussolini's leadership within the Fascist Party.

Ans. (b) They used violence and intimidation against political opponents to create fear and instability.

Q.6 The extract given below refers to Mussolini's rise to power in Italy, where Fascist militias used violence and intimidation against political opponents, leading to the March on Rome in 1922.

The New York Times
Book Review

MUSSOLINI, MASTER OF ITALY

Which of the following democratic principles were ignored during this process?

P : Respect for democratic institutions

Q : Freedom of political opposition

R : Use of peaceful methods in politics

S : Rule of law

(a) P and Q (b) Q and R

(c) P, Q and R (d) R and S

Ans. (c) P, Q and R

Q.7 Identify the main difference between OVRA and the regular police in Fascist Italy.

(a) OVRA was responsible for economic planning, while the regular police managed law and order.

(b) OVRA operated as a secret police to suppress political opposition, while the regular police performed routine policing.

(c) OVRA protected workers' rights, while the regular police supported trade unions.

(d) OVRA worked independently of the Fascist government, while the regular police worked under Mussolini.

Ans. (b) OVRA operated as a secret police to suppress political opposition, while the regular police performed routine policing.

Q.8 Who among the following leaders prioritised economic self-sufficiency (autarky) in Italy?

(a) Victor Emmanuel III (b) Giovanni Giolitti

(c) Benito Mussolini (d) Count Cavour

Ans. (c) Benito Mussolini

Q.9 Which of the following events is considered to be Mussolini's final confirmation of his dictatorship in Italy?

(a) The Signing of the Lateran Treaty (1929)

(b) The March on Rome (1922)

(c) The Formation of the Fascist Party (1919)

(d) The Election of 1921

Ans. (a) The Signing of the Lateran Treaty (1929)

Q.10 Which of the following best reflects a critical assessment of Mussolini's economic policies in Italy?

(a) They successfully made Italy completely self-sufficient and economically strong.

(b) They improved workers' wages and strengthened independent trade unions.

(c) They provided short-term stability but failed to achieve long-term economic growth.

(d) They reduced state control and promoted free-market competition.

Ans. (c) They provided short-term stability but failed to achieve long-term economic growth.

Assertion-Reason Questions

Given below are two statements marked as Assertion (A) are Reason (R). Read the two statements carefully and choose the correct answer from the codes given below.

Codes

(a) Both A and R are true and R is the correct explanation of A.

(b) Both A and R are true, but R is not the correct explanation of A.

(c) A is true, but R is false.

(d) Both A and R are false.

Q.1 Assertion (A) Italy faced severe economic difficulties after World War I, including unemployment and inflation.

Reason (R) Italy had emerged from the war with heavy debts and limited economic resources.

Ans. (a) Both A and R are true and R is the correct explanation of A.

Q.2 Assertion (A) Many Italians lost faith in liberal democracy after World War I.

Reason (R) The parliamentary system failed to deal effectively with economic problems and social unrest.

Ans. (a) Both A and R are true and R is the correct explanation of A.

Q.3 Assertion (A) Mussolini introduced corporatism to reduce conflict between workers and employers.

Reason (R) Corporatism allowed independent trade unions to function freely and protected workers' rights.

Ans. (c) A is true, but R is false.

Q.4 Assertion (A) Mussolini's policy of autarky failed to make Italy economically self-sufficient.

Reason (R) Italy lacked many essential raw materials required for industrial production.

Ans. (a) Both A and R are true and R is the correct explanation of A.

Very Short Answer Type Questions

Q.1 Italians described their post-war experience as a .... because Italy did not receive all promised territories.

Ans. Mutilated victory

Q.2 The March on Rome took place in .... 1922.

Ans. 27th-29th October, 1922

Q.3 The image given below shows a photograph of Benito Mussolini, the Prime Minister of Italy.

Source: Wikimedia Commons

Name the political ideology associated with the leader shown in the image.

Ans. Fascism

Q.4 Between 1921 and 1922, Mussolini organised Fascist militias known as the Blackshirts.

State one way in which the Blackshirts helped Mussolini in his rise to power.

Ans. The Blackshirts used violence and intimidation to suppress political opponents, to creating fear and instability, allowing Mussolini to project himself as a leader capable of re-establishing law and order.

Q.5 King .... refused to declare martial law and invited Mussolini to form the government.

Ans. Victor Emmanuel III

Q.6 The March on Rome in October 1922 forced King Victor Emmanuel III to invite Mussolini to form the government.

What was the significance of this event in Italian politics?

Ans. The March on Rome marked the end of liberal parliamentary rule in Italy and paved the way for the establishment of a Fascist dictatorship under Mussolini.

Q.7 Benito Mussolini became the Prime Minister of Italy in the year ....

Ans. 1922

Q.8 Mussolini established a .... by concentrating power in his own hands.

Ans. Dictatorship

Q.9 Agricultural campaigns such as the .... increased wheat production in Italy.

Ans. Battle for Grain

Q.10 The Fascist Party won .... seats in the parliamentary elections of 1921.

Ans. 35

Q.11 Expand OVRA.

Ans. Organisation for Vigilance and Repression of Anti-Fascism

Q.12 Mention any one measure taken by Mussolini to control public opinion.

Ans. Imposition of strict censorship on the press.

Q.13 Mention any one limitation of Mussolini's economic policies.

Ans. The policies favoured large industries and wealthy industrialists over workers.

TYPE - 2   4 Marks

Short Answer Type Questions

Q.1 With reference to the news extract given below, state any four circumstances that led to the rise of Fascism under Benito Mussolini in Italy.

Source:www.nytimes.com

The New York Times Book Review

MUSSOLINI, MASTER OF ITALY

A New Picture Emerges From His Authorized Biography

Ans. Four circumstances that led to the rise of Fascism under Benito Mussolini in Italy are as follows

(i) After World War I, Italy faced severe economic problems such as unemployment, inflation, and war debts, which caused widespread dissatisfaction among the people.

(ii) The liberal parliamentary government in Italy was weak and unstable, and it failed to deal effectively with economic hardship and social unrest.

(iii) The feeling of a 'mutilated victory' after World War I created nationalist resentment, because Italy did not receive the territories promised to it.

(iv) Fear of a socialist revolution among the middle class, industrialists and landowners increased support for Fascism as it promised strong authoritarian leadership and order.

Q.2 How did the course of events between 1921 and 1922 contribute to Mussolini's rise to power in Italy?

Ans. The course of events between 1921 and 1922 contribute to Mussolini's rise to power in Italy in the following ways

- In the 1921 elections, Mussolini's Fascist Party won 35 seats, establishing themselves as a recognised political force.
- Mussolini organised Blackshirts, who attacked socialists, trade unionists, and political opponents, creating fear and instability.
- The weak coalition governments failed to handle economic hardship, social unrest and strikes, which increased public dissatisfaction.
- The March on Rome in October 1922 forced King Victor Emmanuel III to invite Mussolini to form a government, marking his rise to power.

Q.3 Benito Mussolini established a Fascist dictatorship in Italy after becoming Prime Minister in 1922. In this context, analyse the impact of Mussolini's domestic policies on the political system of Italy.

Ans. The impact of Mussolini's domestic policies on the political system of Italy was as follows

- Mussolini concentrated all political power in his own hands, which led to the destruction of parliamentary democracy in Italy.
- Opposition political parties were banned and freedom of speech was curtailed through strict press censorship, thereby ending political pluralism.
- The establishment of the secret police, OVRA, created a climate of fear and repression, weakening civil liberties and political participation.
- Strong state propaganda and control over education and youth organisations promoted unquestioned loyalty to the Fascist state and Mussolini.

Q.4 Between 1921 and 1922, Mussolini organised Fascist militias known as the Blackshirts, who attacked socialists, trade unionists and political opponents.

With reference to the above extract, state any four ways in which the Blackshirts helped Mussolini in his rise to power.

Ans. Four ways in which the Blackshirts helped Mussolini in his rise to power were

(i) The Blackshirts used violence and intimidation to suppress socialist and communist groups.

(ii) They weakened opposition parties by attacking trade unions and political rivals.

(iii) Their actions created lawlessness and fear, which made the government appear weak and ineffective.

(iv) They helped Mussolini project himself as a strong leader capable of restoring order.

Q.5 Discuss any four achievements of Benito Mussolini to justify his rise as a powerful leader in Italy.

Ans. Four achievements of Benito Mussolini to justify his rise as a powerful leader in Italy were as follows

(i) Mussolini brought political stability to Italy by ending frequent changes of weak coalition governments and establishing a strong central authority.

(ii) He used effective propaganda to promote nationalism and project himself as a dynamic and decisive leader.

(iii) Mussolini launched public works programmes such as road construction and land reclamation which temporarily reduced unemployment.

(iv) The signing of the Lateran Treaty in 1929 improved relations with the Catholic Church and strengthened his popular support.

Q.6 State any two reasons for each that why Mussolini's economic and social policies failed to improve the lives of ordinary Italians.

Ans. Mussolini's economic policies failed to improve the lives of ordinary Italians because

- The policy of Autarky was inefficient because Italy lacked essential raw materials, raising the costs of production.
- Agricultural campaigns like the Battle for Grain reduced cultivation of other crops, harming food diversity.
- Mussolini's social policies failed to improve the lives of ordinary Italians because
- Corporatism primarily benefitted employers leaving workers' wages low and limiting labour rights.
- Unequal industrial growth meant ordinary workers saw little improvement in living standards despite propaganda claims.

TYPE - 3 8 Marks

Long Answer Type Questions

Q.1 In October 1922, when Fascist militias marched, many Italian leaders feared that the country was heading towards chaos and civil war.

Source: Contemporary accounts

(a) Identify the event referred to in the above extract. State any three features of this event.

(b) Discuss any four reasons why King Victor Emmanuel III accepted Mussolini as the Prime Minister of Italy.

Ans. (a) The event referred to in the above extract is the March on Rome (October 1922).

Three features of the March on Rome were

- Nearly 30,000 Fascist 'Blackshirts' marched towards Rome to threaten the seizure of power.
- The march created a serious political crisis and paralysed the functioning of the Italian government.
- The Fascists used the threat of violence rather than a direct military takeover to pressure the authorities.

(b) Four reasons for the acceptance of Mussolini as Prime Minister were:

- King Victor Emmanuel III feared that declaring martial law against the Fascists would lead to a civil war.
- The existing liberal coalition governments were weak and had failed to control economic hardship and social unrest.
- Mussolini was perceived as a strong leader who could restore law and order in the country.
- Many industrialists, landowners, and conservatives supported Mussolini as a safeguard against Socialism and Communism.

Q.2 "Mussolini aimed at making Italy self-sufficient through agricultural campaigns, large public works, and corporatist policies."

Source: Contemporary economic reports, Italy, 1925-30

With reference to Mussolini's economic policies, answer the following questions:

(a) State any four measures adopted by Mussolini to improve the Italian economy.

(b) Discuss any two reasons each for the partial success of Mussolini's economic policies, and their limitations in improving the lives of ordinary Italians.

Ans. (a) Four measures adopted by Mussolini to improve the Italian economy were

- Introduction of corporatism, organising workers and employers into state-controlled corporations to prevent class conflict.
- Launching large public works programmes, such as road construction and land reclamation, to reduce unemployment.
- Promotion of agricultural campaigns like the Battle for Grain to increase domestic food production.
- The Pursuit of autarky was intended to make Italy economically self-sufficient and reduce reliance on imports.

(b) Two reasons for the partial success of Mussolini's economic policies were

- Public works and land reclamation projects temporarily reduced unemployment and improved infrastructure.
- Agricultural campaigns increased wheat production, contributing to short-term food security.

Two reasons for the limitations of Mussolini's economic policies were

- Corporatism primarily benefitted employers and large industrialists, while workers' wages remained low and their trade unions were suppressed.
- Autarky was costly and inefficient because Italy lacked essential raw materials, leaving the economy weak and dependent on imports.

Q.3 **Discuss any eight points on the critical appraise of the policies of Benito Mussolini in Italy.**

Ans. Eight points on the critical appraisal of the policies of Benito Mussolini in Italy were

- Mussolini's economic policies temporarily reduced unemployment through public works programmes such as road construction and land reclamation.
- The policy of corporatism aimed to reduce class conflict, but in practice it favoured employers and limited workers' rights.
- Agricultural campaigns like the Battle for Grain increased wheat production but harmed the cultivation of other important crops, leading to an imbalance in the agriculture sector.
- Industrial growth under Fascism was uneven and primarily benefitted large industries and wealthy industrialists rather than ordinary workers.
- Workers' wages were kept low, and trade unions were controlled by the state, leading to poor living standards for the working class.
- Mussolini's policy of autarky attempted to make Italy economically self-sufficient but proved costly and inefficient due to the lack of essential raw materials.
- Politically, Mussolini created a dictatorship by banning opposition parties, controlling the press, and using the secret police OVRA to suppress dissent, limiting freedom of speech and political participation.
- While propaganda projected an image of economic stability and national revival, Italy remained economically weak, socially unequal, and dependent on imports, reflecting the failure of Mussolini's policies in achieving long-term stability and welfare.

11

RISE OF NAZISM

- After Germany's defeat in World War I, the country faced economic crisis, political instability and social unrest.
- Adolf Hitler emerged as a popular leader who promised to restore national pride, provide jobs and fight communism.
- He used propaganda and mass support and gradually rose to power by 1933.

Adolf Hitler

Weaknesses of the Weimar Republic

- In Germany, the Weimar Republic was politically weak because there were frequent changes in government and many coalition governments were unable to make decisions.
- The Republic was unpopular among the people because of the Treaty of Versailles (1919), which Germany had to accept. The treaty caused territorial losses, demanded heavy reparations and military restrictions, making Germans feel humiliated.
- Germany faced severe economic problems. In 1923, hyperinflation depleted the savings of the middle-class people. Later, the Great Depression (1929) caused mass unemployment and poverty, making life very hard for ordinary citizens.
- The Republic was unable to maintain law and order. Political extremists from both the left (communists) and right (nationalists) were active, and there were many violent clashes the streets.
- Many powerful groups, such as the army, industrialists and conservatives, did not fully support the Weimar Republic. They often hoped for a strong leader who could replace the weak government.
- The system of proportional representation resulted in difficulty in forming a strong government, as too many small parties had seats in the parliament, leading to instability.
- The Weimar Republic was also blamed for Germany's defeat in World War I and the hardships that followed, which made many people feel that the government was not loyal to the nation.
- Ordinary citizens were frustrated because the government seemed unable to solve economic and social problems, which created a sense of hopelessness and anger.

Events Leading to Rise of Hitler

- In July 1932, Germany held Reichstag (parliament) elections.
- The Nazi or NSDAP Party (National Socialist German Workers' Party) became the largest party in the Reichstag and won 230 seats, but they did not have a majority to form the government alone.
- After the elections, Franz von Papen, a conservative politician formed government. Papen's government was weak and could not get support from the Reichstag.
- In November 1932, new elections were held. The Nazi Party lost some seats but still remained the strongest party in the Reichstag. Other parties were unable to form a stable government.
- During this period, Hitler refused to joint the cabinet, insisting that he should be appointed Chancellor only if given full power once appointed. Meanwhile, political instability continued in Germany.
- Conservative politicians, including Franz von Papen and other elites, underestimated Hitler, believing they could manipulate him to stabilise the government while fighting communism.

- After negotiations and pressure from these conservative leaders, President Hindenburg agreed to appoint Hitler as Chancellor.
- On 30th January 1933, Adolf Hitler was officially appointed Chancellor of Germany, marking the beginning of Nazi rule and the eventual end of the Weimar Republic.

Swastika: Symbol of Nazi Party

The Nazi State: From 1933 Onwards

- After being appointed Chancellor in January 1933, Adolf Hitler and the Nazi Party quickly moved to consolidate power in Germany.
- They aimed to establish a totalitarian state where the government controlled all aspects of political, social, and cultural life.

Changes Made by Hitler

Changes in Government

- Hitler and the Nazi Party quickly eliminated all political opposition to establish a one-party state.
- The Reichstag Fire (1933) was used as an excuse to pass the Enabling Act. This gave Hitler the power to make laws without the Reichstag.
- Local governments were brought under Nazi control and all opposition parties were banned by 1934.
- Hitler became the Fuhrer (leader) of Germany after President Hindenburg's death in 1934, combining the roles of Chancellor and President.

Changes in Cultural Life and Education

- The Nazis controlled books, newspapers, films and radio to spread Nazi ideas and propaganda.
- Teachers were required to teach Nazi ideology, including obedience, nationalism and racial purity.
- Schools emphasised physical fitness, military training and loyalty to Hitler.
- Cultural activities, art and music were censored. Only works that supported Nazi ideas were allowed.

Changes in the Army (Night of the Long Knives)

- Hitler wanted to control the army and remove threats within the Nazi Party.
- In June 1934, during the Night of the Long Knives, Hitler ordered the killing of leaders of the SA (Stormtroopers), including Ernst Rohm, was were seen as a threat.
- After this, the army pledged loyalty directly to Hitler, not to Germany or the Constitution.

Changes in the Economy

- Hitler's government aimed to reduce unemployment by launching large-scale public works projects, such as building autobahns (highways).
- The Nazis supported building up the army and weapons, which helped create jobs in factories and for soldiers.
- Trade unions were banned and businesses were brought under state control, while private ownership continued under strict government rules.
- The economy was directed to support military growth and self-sufficiency.

Changes in Religious Life

- Hitler tried to bring churches under Nazi influence through the German Christian Movement.
- Religious leaders who opposed the Nazis were persecuted, arrested or silenced.
- Nazi ideology promoted loyalty to Hitler above religious beliefs.
- Schools and youth organisations promoted nationalist and pagan traditions (beliefs such as nature worship), while allowing only limited, state-controlled Christian teachings.

Escalation of the Nazi Campaign Against the Jews

Early Discrimination (1933-1935)

- Soon after Hitler came to power in 1933, the Nazis began discriminating against Jews in public life.
- Jews were removed from government jobs, teaching positions and the civil service.
- Jewish businesses were boycotted and laws restricted their rights in the economy.

- The Nuremberg Laws (1935) were introduced, which took away German citizenship from Jews and prohibited marriage or sexual relations between Jews and non-Jews.

Increasing Persecution (1936-1938)

- Jews were gradually excluded from the schools, universities and professional jobs.
- Nazi propaganda portrayed Jews as the cause of Germany's problems, spreading hatred among the population.
- Kristallnacht (Night of Broken Glass, 9-10 November 1938) marked a major escalation: Jewish shops, homes and synagogues were destroyed, and thousands of Jews were arrested or killed.

Forced Segregation and Deportation (1939-1941)

- After the outbreak of World War II (1939), the Nazis began the ghettoisation (put in an isolated place) of Jews in occupied territories, especially in Poland.
- Jews were forced to live in overcrowded ghettos, separated from the rest of the population, under harsh conditions.
- Jews were forced to wear identifying badges, like the yellow Star of David, to mark them as targets for discrimination.

Mass Killings and the 'Final Solution' (1941-1945)

- In 1941, Hitler and the Nazi leadership reached a decision on the 'Final Solution', a plan to systematically kill all Jews in Europe.
- Special death squads began mass shootings of Jews in occupied territories.
- Jews were deported to concentration and extermination camps, such as Auschwitz, Treblinka and Sobibor.
- Millions of Jews were killed using gas chambers, starvation, forced labour and executions.
- By the end of World War II in 1945, approximately six million Jews had been murdered in the mass killing.

Extermination Camp

Reasons for Hitler's Popularity and Policies Among Different Groups

Workers and the unemployed people Many workers and unemployed people supported Hitler because he promised to create jobs, reduce unemployment, and improve living conditions during the economic crisis caused by the Great Depression.

Middle class and small businessmen They feared communism and the rise of left-wing parties. They supported Hitler because he promised law, order and protection of private property.

Farmers They suffered from low crop prices and economic difficulties. They supported Hitler because he promised higher agricultural prices and protection for their farms.

Industrialists and business elites They supported Hitler as he was a strong anti-communist leader who could protect their businesses and property from strikes and socialist policies.

Youth and students They were attracted to Hitler because of his speeches, mass rallies, and promises to restore national pride. They believed he could make Germany strong and respected again.

Nationalists and veterans They supported Hitler because he promised to overturn the Treaty of Versailles, rebuild Germany's military strength and restore national honour.

General public Hitler became popular with ordinary citizens because he spoke in accessible language, used effective propaganda, and offered solutions to Germany's economic, social and political problems.

EXAM ORIENTED QUESTIONS

TYPE - 1 1 Mark

Multiple Choice Questions

Q.1 "The Treaty of Versailles caused territorial losses, heavy reparations and military restrictions on German people"

Which sentiment among Germans was mainly responsible for increasing support for Nazism?

(a) Satisfaction (b) National humiliation
(c) Political instability (d) Economic growth

Ans. (b) National humiliation

Q.2 Identify the key difference between the Weimar Republic and the Nazi State in Germany.

(a) The Weimar Republic promoted a one-party dictatorship, while the Nazi State followed democratic principles.
(b) The Nazi State upheld parliamentary democracy, while the Weimar Republic abolished elections.
(c) The Weimar Republic was a democratic system, while the Nazi State was a totalitarian dictatorship.
(d) Both the Weimar Republic and the Nazi State followed identical political systems.

Ans. (c) The Weimar Republic was a democratic system, while the Nazi State was a totalitarian dictatorship.

Q.3 Which of the following developments best explains why conservative leaders supported Adolf Hitler's appointment as Chancellor in 1933?

(a) They believed Hitler would immediately restore democratic institutions.
(b) They expected to control Hitler and use him to stabilise the government while opposing communism.
(c) They supported Hitler's racial ideology and anti-Jewish policies.
(d) They feared the growing influence of the Weimar Constitution.

Ans. (b) They expected to control Hitler and use him to stabilise the government while opposing communism.

Q.4 Which position did Adolf Hitler finally obtain on 30th January, 1933?

(a) President of Germany (b) Chief of the Army
(c) Chancellor of Germany (d) Head of the Reichstag

Ans. (c) Chancellor of Germany

Q.5 Who among the following Presidents appointed Adolf Hitler as the Chancellor of Germany in 1933?

(a) Wilhelm II
(b) Paul von Hindenburg
(c) Otto von Bismarck
(d) Franz von Papen

Ans. (b) Paul von Hindenburg

Q.6 The following image depicts Adolf Hitler addressing a massive public rally in Germany after his appointment as Chancellor in 1933.

Which one of the following best explains how such events helped Hitler strengthen his control over Germany?

(a) They promoted free political debate and opposition.
(b) They encouraged democratic decision-making.
(c) They used propaganda and emotional appeal to unite people behind Nazi ideology.
(d) They reduced the role of the state in public life.

Ans. (c) They used propaganda and emotional appeal to unite people behind Nazi ideology.

Q.7 Identify the key difference between Hitler's economic policies and the Weimar Republic's economic approach.

(a) Hitler reduced state control, while the Weimar Republic controlled all industries.
(b) Hitler focused on rearmament and public works whereas the Weimar Republic had struggled with economic crises.
(c) Both followed identical economic policies.
(d) The Weimar Republic had achieved complete economic stability, while Hitler caused unemployment.

Ans. (b) Hitler focused on rearmament and public works whereas the Weimar Republic had struggled with economic crises.

Q.8 "The Reichstag Fire was used as an excuse to pass the Enabling Act, giving Hitler the power to make laws without the Reichstag."

What was the main result of the Enabling Act (1933)?

(a) Restoration of democracy.
(b) Strengthening of Parliament.
(c) Establishment of one-party rule.
(d) Expansion of civil liberties.

Ans. (c) Establishment of one-party rule.

Q.9 The extract given below highlights the use of the Enabling Act (1933), which allowed Adolf Hitler to rule without the approval of the Reichstag.

Source : Enabling Act (1933), Wikipedia

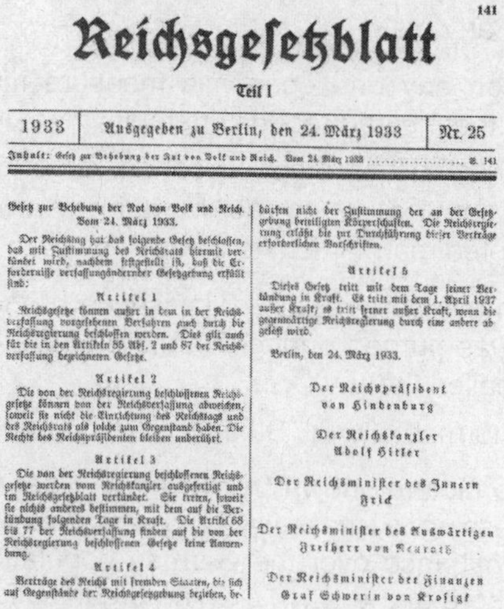

141

Reichsgesetzblatt

Teil I

1933	Ausgegeben zu Berlin, den 24. März 1933	Nr. 25

Inhalt: Gesetz zur Behebung der Not von Volk und Reich. Vom 24. März 1933 .... S. 141

Gesetz zur Behebung der Not von Volk und Reich. Vom 24. März 1933.

Der Reichstag hat das folgende Gesetz beschlossen, das mit Zustimmung des Reichsrats hiermit verkündet wird, nachdem festgestellt ist, daß die Erfordernisse verfassungändernder Gesetzgebung erfüllt sind:

Artikel 1

Reichsgesetze können außer in dem in der Reichsverfassung vorgesehenen Verfahren auch durch die Reichsregierung beschlossen werden. Dies gilt auch für die in den Artikeln 85 Abs. 2 und 87 der Reichsverfassung bezeichneten Gesetze.

Artikel 2

Die von der Reichsregierung beschlossenen Reichsgesetze können von der Reichsverfassung abweichen, soweit sie nicht die Einrichtung des Reichstags und des Reichsrats als solche zum Gegenstand haben. Die Rechte des Reichspräsidenten bleiben unberührt.

Artikel 3

Die von der Reichsregierung beschlossenen Reichsgesetze werden vom Reichskanzler ausgefertigt und im Reichsgesetzblatt verkündet. Sie treten, soweit sie nichts anderes bestimmen, mit dem auf die Verkündung folgenden Tage in Kraft. Die Artikel 68 bis 77 der Reichsverfassung finden auf die von der Reichsregierung beschlossenen Gesetze keine Anwendung.

Artikel 4

Verträge des Reichs mit fremden Staaten, die sich auf Gegenstände der Reichsgesetzgebung beziehen, bedürfen nicht der Zustimmung der an der Gesetzgebung beteiligten Körperschaften. Die Reichsregierung erläßt die zur Durchführung dieser Verträge erforderlichen Vorschriften.

Artikel 5

Dieses Gesetz tritt mit dem Tage seiner Verkündung in Kraft. Es tritt mit dem 1. April 1937 außer Kraft; es tritt ferner außer Kraft, wenn die gegenwärtige Reichsregierung durch eine andere abgelöst wird.

Berlin, den 24. März 1933.

Der Reichspräsident
von Hindenburg

Der Reichskanzler
Adolf Hitler

Der Reichsminister des Innern
Frick

Der Reichsminister des Auswärtigen
Freiherr von Neurath

Der Reichsminister der Finanzen
Graf Schwerin von Krosigk

Which of the following democratic principles of the Weimar Constitution were ignored due to this act?

P : Separation of powers
Q : Rule of law
R : Parliamentary democracy
S : Judicial independence

(a) P and R
(b) Q and S
(c) P, Q and R
(d) R and S

Ans. (c) P, Q and R

Q.10 The Nuremberg Laws (1935) took away German citizenship from Jews and prohibited marriage between Jews and non-Jews.

What was Hitler's main objective behind the Night of the Long Knives?

(a) To please foreign powers.
(b) To gain support of farmers.
(c) To remove internal threats and control the army.
(d) To expand Germany's borders.

Ans. (c) To remove internal threats and control the army.

Q.11 Identify the key difference between the Nuremberg Laws and the Enabling Act.

(a) Both aimed at economic recovery.
(b) The Enabling Act strengthened parliamentary democracy, while the Nuremberg Laws restricted political parties.
(c) The Enabling Act gave Hitler dictatorial powers, while the Nuremberg Laws targeted Jews on racial grounds.
(d) Both were introduced to reduce unemployment.

Ans. (c) The Enabling Act gave Hitler dictatorial powers, while the Nuremberg Laws targeted Jews on racial grounds.

Q.12 Which of the following changes best illustrates Hitler's aim to establish a one-party totalitarian state in Germany?

(a) Launch of public works programmes.
(b) Banning of all opposition political parties.
(c) Introduction of agricultural subsidies.
(d) Promotion of youth organisations.

Ans. (b) Banning of all opposition political parties.

Q.13 Which of the following measures best indicate the shift from legal discrimination to open violence against Jews in Nazi Germany?

(a) Boycott of Jewish businesses.
(b) Dismissal of Jews from government services.
(c) Introduction of the Nuremberg Laws.
(d) Kristallnacht (Night of Broken Glass), 1938.

Ans. (d) Kristallnacht (Night of Broken Glass), 1938

Q.14 Which of the following developments best demonstrates the transition from persecution to systematic extermination of Jews by the Nazi regime?

(a) Exclusion of Jews from schools and universities.
(b) Formation of Jewish ghettos in occupied territories.
(c) Decision to implement the 'Final Solution' in 1941.
(d) Nazi propaganda against Jews.

Ans. (c) Decision to implement the 'Final Solution' in 1941.

Assertion-Reason Questions

Given below are two statements marked as Assertion (A) and Reason (R). Read the two statements carefully and choose the correct answer from the codes given below.

Codes

(a) Both A and R are true and R is the correct explanation of A.
(b) Both A and R are true, but R is not the correct explanation of A.
(c) A is true, but R is false.
(d) Both A and R are false.

Q.1 Assertion (A) The Weimar Republic was politically weak due to frequent changes in government.

Reason (R) The system of proportional representation led to coalition governments and instability.

Ans. (a) Both A and R are true and R is the correct explanation of A.

Q.2 Assertion (A) Adolf Hitler was able to pass laws only with the approval of the Reichstag after 1933.

Reason (R) The Nuremberg Act was passed following the Reichstage Fire.

Ans. (d) Both A and R are false.

Q.3 Assertion (A) The Night of the Long Knives strengthened Hitler's position as the leader of Germany.

Reason (R) It removed the leadership of the SA thereby securing the loyalty of the army.

Ans. (a) Both A and R are true and R is the correct explanation of A.

Q.4 Assertion (A) Nazi control over education and culture was used to spread obedience, nationalism, and loyalty to Hitler among Germans.

Reason (R) Teachers were required to teach Nazi ideology and only approved books, art, and music were allowed.

Ans. (a) Both A and R are true and R is the correct explanation of A.

Q.5 Assertion (A) The Nazi campaign against the Jews intensified after the outbreak of the Second World War.

Reason (R) Jews were forced into ghettos and later deported to extermination camps.

Ans. (a) Both A and R are true and R is the correct explanation of A.

Very Short Answer Type Questions

Q.1 Expand NSDAP.

Ans. National Socialist German Workers' Party

Q.2 "After being appointed Chancellor in January 1933, Adolf Hitler and the Nazi Party quickly moved to consolidate power and establish a totalitarian state."

What was the significance of Hitler's consolidation of power in Germany?

Ans. It marked the end of the Weimar Republic, which allowed Hitler to control all political, social and cultural life, and enabled the implementation of Nazi policies, including persecution of Jews and suppression of opposition.

Q.3 The image given below shows a symbol of Hitler's party.

Source: www.wikipedia.org

Name the political party of Hitler represented by this symbol.

Ans. National Socialist German Workers' Party (NSDAP)/ Nazi Party

Q.4 Mention any one economic measure introduced by Hitler that helped reduce unemployment in Germany.

Ans. The Nazi government launched large public works programmes, such as building Autobahns and promoted rearmament to create jobs.

Q.5 The mass paramilitary organisation of the Nazi Party that was purged during the Night of the Long Knives was called the ....

Ans. SA (Sturmabteilung / Stormtroopers)

Q.6 In the picture shown below, Adolf Hitler can be seen addressing a mass rally, demonstrating his power and influence over the German population, including members of the ...., the organisation created to indoctrinate German youth in Nazi ideology.

Source:historyextra.com

Ans. Hitler Youth (Hitlerjugend)

Q.7 "Soon after Hitler came to power in 1933, Jews were removed from government jobs, teaching positions and the civil service. Jewish businesses were boycotted, and laws restricted their rights in the economy."

Source: Escalation of the Nazi campaign against the Jews, 193

State any one impact this event had on the lives of Jews in Germany.

Ans. Jews lost their jobs, were economically boycotted, and faced social and legal discrimination, making them marginalised and deprived of basic rights in German society.

Q.8 **The policy of forcing Jews to live in isolated areas under harsh conditions after 1939 was called ....**

Ans. Ghettoisation

TYPE - 2   4 Marks

Short Answer Type Questions

Q.1 **With reference to the text above, state any four weaknesses of the Weimar Republic that contributed to the rise of Nazism in Germany.**

Source: www.nytimes.com

Are There Lessons in the Weimar Republic?

Perhaps, but two studies of Germany back then demonstrate why its crises pale in comparison.

GERMANY AFTER THE FIRST WORLD WAR

THE GREAT DISORDER

By Richard J. Evans

The depression now in a reunified Germany makes one see ghosts of the economic chaos of the 1920's and the fascism

Ans. Four weaknesses of the Weimar Republic that contributed to the rise of Nazism in Germany were as follows

(i) The Weimar Republic was politically weak due to frequent changes in government and unstable coalition administrations that could not take strong decisions.

(ii) The Treaty of Versailles caused territorial losses, heavy reparations and military restrictions, which made the Republic unpopular among the German people.

(iii) Severe economic crises, such as hyperinflation in 1923 and mass unemployment during the Great Depression, resulted in widespread poverty and frustration.

(iv) The Republic failed to maintain law and order, as political extremists from both the left and right were active, resulting in frequent violent clashes.

Q.2 **After being appointed Chancellor in January 1933, Adolf Hitler and the Nazi Party quickly consolidated power. They banned opposition parties, controlled the media, and used propaganda to gain public support.**

Source:Historical Records

Based on the above report, state any four reasons for Hitler's rise to power.

Ans. Four reasons far Hitler's rise to power were as follows

(i) Politically the Weimer Republic was unstable and weak; the frequent changes in government paved the way to Hitler to rise to the power.

(ii) Economic crises, and mass unemployment during the Great Depression, created widespread frustration among ordinary citizens.

(iii) Many conservative elites and industrialists supported Hitler, believing they could control him and use his leadership to protect their interests and fight communism.

(iv) Hitler's use of propaganda, mass rallies and promises to restore national pride, provide jobs, and overturn the Treaty of Versailles won him widespread public support.

Q.3 **State any four reasons for Hitler's popularity among different groups in Germany during his rise to power.**

Ans. Four reasons for Hitler's popularity among different groups in Germany during his rise to power were as follows

(i) Many workers and unemployed people supported Hitler because he promised jobs, reduced unemployment, and improved living conditions during the economic crisis caused by the Great Depression.

(ii) Middle-class citizens and small business owners supported Hitler as he promised law, order, and protection of property from communist influence.

(iii) Farmers supported Hitler because he promised higher agricultural prices, subsidies and protection for their farms.

(iv) Youth and students were attracted to Hitler's speeches, mass rallies, and promises to restore national pride and re-establish Germany as a formidable global power.

Q.4 **Adolf Hitler was appointed Chancellor of Germany on 30th January, 1933. He soon used the Reichstag Fire and the Enabling Act to consolidate power and eliminate political opposition.**

In the above context, analyse the impact of Hitler's rise on the democratic system in Germany.

Ans. The impact of Hitler's rise on the democratic system in Germany were as follows

- Hitler's appointment marked the end of the Weimar Republic and the collapse of democracy in Germany.
- The Reichstag Fire and the Enabling Act allowed Hitler to pass laws without parliamentary approval, effectively bypassing democratic processes.
- All political opposition was banned and Germany became a one-party state under Nazi control.
- The combination of the offices of Chancellor and President after Hindenburg's death concentrated power in Hitler's hands, establishing a totalitarian regime.
- Democratic institutions, such as free elections and independent legislative authority, were destroyed, and citizens lost political freedoms.

Q.5 Discuss any four changes made by Hitler in cultural life and education in Germany after 1933.

Ans. Four changes made by Hitler in cultural life and education in Germany after 1933 were as follows

(i) The Nazis exercised control over books, newspapers, films, and radio to spread Nazi propaganda and influence public opinion.

(ii) Teachers were required to teach Nazi ideology, including obedience, nationalism and racial purity.

(iii) Schools emphasised physical fitness, military training and loyalty to Hitler to prepare youth for the Nazi state.

(iv) Cultural activities, art, and music were censored, allowing only works that promoted Nazi values and suppressed opposing ideas.

Q.6 State any two features of the changes in the army and government introduced by Hitler after becoming Chancellor. Mention any two reasons to explain why these changes helped him consolidate power in Germany.

Ans. Two features of changes in army and the government by Hitler were as follows

(i) The Night of the Long Knives (June 1934) eliminated leaders of the SA, including Ernst Rohm, perceived as a threat to Hitler's authority.

(ii) After President Hindenburg's death in 1934, Hitler combined the offices of Chancellor and President, becoming the Fuhrer, and centralised all executive power in his hands.

The changes which helped Hitler to consolidate power were as follows

(i) The army pledged direct loyalty to Hitler rather than to Germany or the Constitution, ensuring military support for his regime.

(ii) Eliminating opposition within the Nazi Party and concentrating power prevented any challenges to Hitler, allowing him to establish a totalitarian government.

Q.7 How did Hitler's policies gain acceptance among different groups in Germany during his rule? Explain with reference to workers, middle-class citizens, farmers, and industrialists.

Ans. Hitler's policies gained acceptance among different groups in the following ways

- Hitler's economic policies, such as large public works programme and rearmament, created employment opportunities and reduced joblessness,, which garnered support from the working class and the unemployed.
- Middle-class citizens and small business owners supported Hitler because he promised law, order, and protection of private property, which reassured them amids fears of communist influence.
- Farmers welcomed Hitler's policies of subsidies, price supports, and protectionist measures, which improved their economic conditions during a period of low crop prices and financial hardship.
- Wealthy industrialists and elites accepted Hitler's policies because he was strongly anti-communist, reduced the risk of strikes and socialist policies, and provided political stability, ensuring both profit and security for their businesses.

TYPE - 3

8 Marks

Long Answer Type Questions

Q.1 Discuss any eight features of the events from 1932 onwards that led to Adolf Hitler becoming Chancellor of Germany.

Ans. Eight features of the events from 1932 onwards that led to Adolf Hitler becoming Chancellor of Germany were as follows

(i) In July 1932, Germany held Reichstag elections in which the Nazi Party became the largest party, winning 230 seats, but without a majority to form the government alone.

(ii) President Hindenburg asked Franz von Papen, a conservative politician, to form a government, but his administration was weak and could not get parliamentary support.

(iii) New elections were held in November 1932; the Nazi Party lost some seats but remained the strongest party in the Reichstag.

(iv) Other political parties were unable to form a stable government due to frequent disagreements and the coalition instability.

(v) Hitler refused to become Chancellor immediately, insisting that he be given full powers once appointed.

(vi) Conservative politicians, including Franz von Papen and other elites, believed they could control Hitler and use him to stabilise Germany while combating communism.

(vii) Negotiations and sustained political pressure from conservative leaders convinced President Hindenburg to appoint Hitler as Chancellor.

(viii) On 30th January 1933, Adolf Hitler was officially appointed Chancellor, marking the start of Nazi rule and the end of the Weimar Republic.

Q.2 **In June 1934, Hitler ordered the killing of Ernst Rohm and other SA leaders to consolidate control over the army.** *Source : Historical Records*

(a) Identify the event mentioned above and state any three features of this event.

(b) Discuss any four reasons why this event helped Hitler consolidate power in Germany.

Ans. (a) The event is called the Night of the Long Knives.

Three features of this event are

- Hitler targeted the leaders of the SA, including Ernst Rohm, who were seen as a threat to his authority.
- The killings were carried out by the Schutzstaftel and other loyal Nazi forces over several days.
- The army pledged direct loyalty to Hitler after this purge, instead of to Germany or its Constitution.

(b) This event helped Hitler consolidate power in Germany in of the following ways

- It eliminated internal threats within the Nazi Party, thereby, strengthening Hitler's control.
- The army's loyalty was secured, ensuring support from Germany's most powerful military institution.
- Conservative elites and industrialists were reassured that Hitler could maintain order and stability.
- The event demonstrated Hitler's decisiveness and ability to deal with opposition, increasing his political authority and public support.

Q.3 **"This is the path to purify the German nation and restore its strength - the Jews are our enemy and must be removed from society."**

Excerpt from Nazi propaganda, 1 '35-1938

With reference to Nazi Germany, answer the following questions.

(a) State any four measures taken by the Nazis to discriminate against Jews before World War II.

(b) Discuss any two reasons each for the intensification of Nazi persecution of Jews and the impact it had on Jewish communities.

Ans. (a) Four measures taken by the Nazis to discriminate against Jews before World War II were

(i) Jews were removed from government jobs, teaching positions and the civil service.

(ii) Jewish businesses were boycotted and legislation was enacted to restrict their economic rights.

(iii) The Nuremberg Laws of 1935 deprived Jews of German citizenship and prohibited marriage or sexual relations between Jews and non-Jews.

(iv) Jews were gradually excluded from schools, universities and professional jobs.

(b) Two impacts of the intensification of Nazi persecution on Jewish communities were

(i) Nazi propaganda falsely portrayed Jews as the cause of Germany's economic and social problems, spreading hatred among ordinary citizens.

(ii) Hitler's government aimed to establish a totalitarian state based on racial purity, making the removal of Jews a key ideological goal.

Two impact of intensification of Nazi persecution on Jewish communities were

(i) Jews were forced to live in overcrowded ghettos and wear identifying badges, such as the yellow Star of David.

(ii) Many Jews were arrested, killed or eventually deported to concentration and extermination camps, leading to the loss of property, freedom and life.

12

RISE OF MILITARISM IN JAPAN

Japanese Militarism

- After World War I, Japan emerged as a modern industrial and military power in Asia. However, during the 1920s and 1930s, the country faced severe economic problems, political instability and social unrest. These difficulties weakened democratic governments and allowed the military to gain influence.
- By the 1930s, Japan's politics and society became dominated by militarism, aggressive nationalism, and expansionist policies, which eventually led to war in Asia.

Background : Rise of Militarism

- **Economic Growth and Industrialisation** Japan industrialised rapidly after World War I and became a major exporter of goods. which created a strong military-industrial sector.
- **Political Instability** The parliamentary system in Japan was inherently weak. Frequent changes in government and political corruption made the civilian government appear incapable of solving national problems.
- **Social Unrest** Rapid industrialisation led to urban crowding, unemployment and worker strikes. Farmers and common people faced hardship, which created dissatisfaction with civilian rule.

Key Events Leading to Militarism

- **Manchurian Crisis (1931)** Officers of the Japanese Army invaded Manchuria without government approval, establishing the puppet state of Manchukuo. This showed that the military could act independently of civilian authority.
- **Suppression of Opposition** Political leaders and socialists who opposed military policies were suppressed and military leaders gained more power over national policy.
- **Expansion in China (1937)** Japan launched the Second Sino-Japanese War, demonstrating complete military dominance in foreign and domestic affairs.

Reasons for the Rise of Militarism in Japan in the 1930s

Economic Crisis

- The Great Depression of 1929 caused severe economic problems in Japan. Exports dropped, factories closed and many people lost their jobs.
- The economic hardship rendered the civilian government ineffective and unable to solve the problems, giving the military an opportunity to gain support.

Imperial Japan

Weak Democratic Government

- Japan's democratic system was unstable. Political parties were often corrupt and governments changed frequently.
- People began to lose faith in democracy and started believing that the military could provide stronger leadership.

REVISION NOTES

Influence and Power of the Military

- The army and navy became very powerful in politics.
- Military leaders believed that Japan's survival depended on strengthening the armed forces and expanding into other territories. They often forced the civilian government to follow their plans.

Extreme Nationalism and Imperial Ambitions

- The military promoted strong nationalism and the idea that Japan should dominate Asia.
- They believed that territorial expansion was necessary to secure raw materials, land, and resources for Japan's growing population and industries.

Fear of Western Powers

- Japan feared that Western countries would dominate Asia and weaken Japan's position.
- Military leaders argued that expansion and a strong army were needed to protect the nation and assert equality with Western powers.

Social Unrest and Public Support

- Unemployment, poverty and strikes caused dissatisfaction among the people.
- The military promised stability, order and national unity, which made their leadership more acceptable to the public.

Propaganda and Emperor Worship

- The military used propaganda to glorify the emperor and promote loyalty to the nation.
- Schools and media were used to teach obedience and nationalism, which made militaristic ideas popular among young people and society in general.

EXAM ORIENTED QUESTIONS

TYPE - 1 — 1 Mark

Multiple Choice Questions

Q.1 "The Great Depression of 1929 caused severe economic problems in Japan. The economic hardship made the civilian government appear weak and unable to solve the problems, giving the military an opportunity to gain support."

Identify the immediate impact of the Great Depression on Japan?

(a) Increase in agricultural production.
(b) Rise in foreign trade.
(c) Closure of factories and unemployment.
(d) Strengthening of democratic governments.

Ans. (c) Closure of factories and unemployment.

Q.2 The following is a picture of militarism in Japan, during the 1930s, a period when democratic governments became weakened and the military gained dominance over politics and society.

Source: Japanese Militarism

Which one of the following best explains why militarism became dominant in Japan during this period?

(a) The success of democratic reforms after World War I.
(b) The ability of civilian governments to solve economic problems.
(c) Economic crisis, political instability and growing influence of the military.
(d) Strong commitment to international peace treaties.

Ans. (c) Economic crisis, political instability and growing influence of the military.

Q.3 Which of the following actions of Japan best reflects the ideas promoted by Japanese militarism during the 1930s?

Source: https://www.alamy.com

News Chronicle

JAPAN'S STARTLING MOVE IN MANCHUKUO

Scheme To Establish Vital Oil Monopoly

THREE NATIONS PROTEST

Britain, United States and Holland

RENEWED THREAT TO NAVAL TALKS

LIFEBOATS IN GALE

MAN BLOWN INTO SEA

HITLER REBUFFS NAZI PRIMATE

RUNAWAY ARMY

SUSPECT IN SHOP CUT WITH RAZOR

P : Use of military force to expand territory
Q : Respect for civilian authority and democracy
R : Promotion of aggressive nationalism
S : Commitment to international peace and treaties

(a) P and R (b) Q and S (c) P and S (d) Q and R

Ans. (a) P and R

Q.4 Which of the following events is considered the clearest demonstration of the Japanese military's dominance over civilian authority in the 1930s?

(a) Rapid industrial growth after World War I
(b) The invasion of Manchuria and the creation of Manchukuo
(c) Political instability
(d) Use of propaganda and Emperor worship

Ans. (b) Invasion of Manchuria and creation of Manchukuo

Q.5 Identify the key difference between democratic government and militarist rule in Japan during the 1930s.

(a) Democratic governments encouraged military expansion, while militarist rule opposed it.
(b) Democratic governments relied on international treaties, while militarist rule advocated aggressive expansion.
(c) Militarist rule strengthened civilian control, while democratic governments undermined it.
(d) Democratic governments supported army independence, while militarist rule limited military power.

Ans. (b) Democratic governments relied on international treaties, while militarist rule promoted aggressive expansion.

Assertion-Reason Questions

Given below are two statements marked as Assertion (A) and Reason (R). Read the two statements carefully and choose the correct answer from the codes given below.

Codes

(a) Both A and R are true and R is correct explanation of A.
(b) Both A and R are true, but R is not the correct explanation of A.
(c) A is true, but R is false.
(d) Both A and R are false.

Q.1 Assertion (A) The Great Depression of 1929 weakened democratic governments in Japan.

Reason (R) The economic crisis caused only unemployment and factory closures.

Ans. (c) A is true, but R is false.

Q.2 Assertion (A) The Manchurian Crisis of 1931 showed that the Japanese military was independent of civilian control.

Reason (R) Japanese army officers invaded Manchuria without government approval and established the puppet state of Manchukuo.

Ans. (a) Both A and R are true and R is correct explanation of A.

Q.3 Assertion (A) Propaganda and Emperor worship played an important role in spreading militaristic ideas in Japan.

Reason (R) Schools and media promoted obedience, loyalty, and nationalism among the people.

Ans. (a) Both A and R are true and R is correct explanation of A.

Very Short Answer Type Questions

Q.1 The invasion of Manchuria by Japanese army officers in 1931 took place without the approval of the ....

Ans. Civilian Government

Q.2 The image given below represents Japanese soldiers marching during the expansion of Japan into China in 1937.

Source: Imperial Japan

Name the war that marked the beginning of Japan's full-scale military expansion in China.

Ans. The Second Sino-Japanese War (1937)

Q.3 Expand SSJW

Ans. Second Sino-Japanese War

Q.4 In 1931, Japanese army officers invaded Manchuria without the approval of the government and set up the puppet state of Manchukuo. *Source: given text*

State any one impact this event had on Japan's political system in the 1930s.

Ans. It strengthened the power and independence of the military over the civilian government.

Q.5 During the 1930s, the Japanese military used propaganda, Emperor worship, and education to promote obedience, nationalism and loyalty to the nation. *Source: Historical records*

What was the significance of this strategy in the rise of militarism in Japan?

Ans. This strategy helped the military gain widespread public support, especially among the younger generation.

TYPE - 2   4 Marks

Short Answer Type Questions

Q.1 With reference to the news extract given below, state any four conditions that helped the rise of militarism in Japan after World War I.

MILITARISM IN JAPAN

Analyze the political and socio-economic factors responsible for the rise of Japanese militarism. Would it be correct to characterize Japanese militarism as 'fascism'?

Introduction. Japan in between 1919 and 1932 faced a number of challenges which lead to the rise of a military government. Japan was faced with a wide range of political, economic and social challenges. There were many reasons which lead to the opting for militarisation of Japan such as the great depression, lack of raw materials and markets for Japanese industries, the corrupt nature of party government, discrimination by western powers and fear of western domination still existed in Japan. Because Japan had a long military tradition, the military was trusted by the people, and the government needed colonies to be able to acquire resources and markets and also in order to attain a degree of equality with the western powers. According to Beeks dictionary the term Militarisation, "is a country's desire to strengthen their armed forces in order to make themselves more powerful." Thus these political and socio-economic challenges that Japan faced appeared to many that they could be solved only by the militarisation of Japan and it was believed that only after that could Japan have colonies, only then could Japan be free from threats of western domination, only then could Japan be able to be respected by the western powers on equal terms. Many people believed that party government of Japan had proved incapable of dealing with the challenges that Japan was facing during this period. Consequently, militarisation became a desired option.

Ans. Four conditions that helped the growth of militarism in Japan after World War I were as follows

(i) After World War I, Japan experienced rapid economic growth and industrialisation, which strengthened its military-industrial complex.

(ii) Japan's democratic system was weak, with frequent changes in government and political corruption.

(iii) Rapid industrialisation caused social problems such as unemployment, urban crowding and labour strikes.

(iv) The failure of civilian governments to solve economic and social problems increased dissatisfaction among the people.

Q.2 **State two reasons for each on the basis of economic crisis and fear of Western power for the rise of militarism in Japan.**

Ans. The reasons with regard to the economic crisis for the rise of militarism in Japan were as follows

(i) The Great Depression of 1929 caused factories to close and many people lost their jobs, making the civilian administration appear weak.

(ii) Economic hardship and unemployment led the people to support the military, believing it could provide stability and strong leadership.

The reasons with regard to the fear of Western power as the reason for the rise of militarism in Japan were as follows

(i) Japan feared that Western countries would dominate Asia and threaten its position in the region.

(ii) Military leaders argued that Japan needed a strong army and territorial expansion to protect the nation and assert equality with Western powers.

Q.3 **How did Japan's extreme nationalism and imperial ambitions contribute to the rise of militarism in the 1930s?**

Ans. Japan's extreme nationalism and imperial ambitions contributed to the rise of 1930s militarism through in the following factors

- Japanese militarists promoted extreme nationalism, creating pride in the nation and a belief in Japan's superiority over other Asian countries.
- Imperial ambitions justified territorial expansion, as Japan needed raw materials, land, and resources to support its growing population and industries.
- Expansionist policies allowed the military to dominate foreign and domestic affairs, weakening civilian government control.
- The combination of nationalism and imperial ambitions increased public support for military leadership, making militarism the dominant political system.

TYPE - 3 — 8 Marks

Long Answer Type Questions

Q.1 After World War I, Japan faced severe economi[c] problems, political instability and social unres[t]. These conditions weakened democrati[c] governments. *Source: Historical Recor[ds]*

(a) Identify the political system that emerged i[n] Japan during the 1930s. State any three feature[s] of this system.

(b) Discuss any four reasons for the acceptance [of] militarism by the Japanese people.

Ans. (a) The political system that emerged in 1930s Japa[n] was known as militarism.

The three features of militarism system were as follow[s]

(i) The military gained control over politic[al] decision-making and weakened civilian authority.

(ii) Aggressive nationalism was promoted to unite th[e] people and support expansion.

(iii) Expansionist foreign policies were followed [to] increase Japan's power in Asia.

(b) Four reasons behind the public's acceptance [of] militarism by the Japanese people are as follows

(i) The Great Depression of 1929 cause[d] unemployment, poverty and economic hardshi[p] making the civilian government appear weak.

(ii) Frequent changes in government and politic[al] corruption led to a loss of faith in democracy.

(iii) The military promised stability, strong leadersh[ip] and national unity during a time of crisis.

(iv) The use of propaganda and emperor worsh[ip] encouraged obedience, nationalism, and support f[or] military rule.

Q.2 **"The survival of Japan depends on a strong arm[y] and expansion into Asia."**

Source: Historical records of Japanese military, 193[0]

With reference to Japanese militarism, answer th[e] following questions

(a) State any four key events or policies th[at] strengthened militarism in Japan.

(b) Discuss any two reasons, each for the stro[ng] influence of the Japanese military and the wea[k] position of the civilian government.

Ans. (a) Four key events or policies that strengthened militarism in Japan were as follows

(i) The invasion of Manchuria in 1931 by the Japanese army officers without government approval.

(ii) Establishment of the puppet state of Manchukuo in Manchuria.

(iii) The expansion into China in 1937, which marked the beginning of the Second Sino-Japanese War.

(iv) The use of propaganda and Emperor worship to promote loyalty and obedience among the people.

(b) Two reasons for the strong influence of the Japanese military were as follows

(i) The military leaders often acted independently, as evidenced by the invasion of Manchuria in 1931.

(ii) Propaganda and Emperor worship increased public support and obedience to the military.

Two reasons for the weak position of the civilian government were

(i) Frequent changes in the government and political corruption made the democratic system unstable.

(ii) Social unrest, poverty, and strikes created widespread dissatisfaction, reducing people's faith in civilian leaders.

Sample Question Paper

SAMPLE QUESTION PAPER (SOLVED)

HISTORY XI

General Instructions

Maximum Marks : 80

Time allowed : Two hours

You are allowed **an additional 15 minutes** for **only** reading the question paper.

You must **NOT** start writing during reading time.

There are **three** sections in the paper; **A**, **B** and **C**. **Internal choices** have been provided in **two questions** each in **Sections B** and **C**.

Answer **all** questions.

While answering **Multiple Choice Questions** in **Section A**, you are required to write **ONLY** one option as the answer.

Section A consists of **one question** each subpart carrying **one mark**.

Section B consists of **eight questions** each carrying **four marks**.

Section C consists of **four questions** each carrying **eight marks**.

The intended marks for questions are given in brackets ().

Section - A

(16 Marks)

Question 1

(i) "The introduction of railways in India transformed the movement of goods and people, linking distant regions and facilitating colonial trade." **(Recall) (1)**

Identify the means of transport referred to in the statement.

(a) Canals (b) Railways (c) Highways (d) Air transport

(ii) Who among the following fought against untouchability and promoted social equality among all castes in Kerala? **(Recall) (1)**

(a) Narayan Guru (b) Jyotirao Phule (c) Veerasalingam (d) Ishwar Chandra Vidyasagar

(iii) Which of the following tribal uprisings between 1899-1900 was led by Birsa Munda against British interference in land rights and traditional governance? **(Evaluate) (1)**

(a) Santhal Rebellion (b) Indigo Uprising

(c) Munda Uprising (d) Deccan Riots

(iv) The following poster shows people boycotting British goods and promoting indigenous products durin
the early 20th century. (

Which one of the following best describes the impact of the movement? **(Evaluat**

(a) It strengthened the British economy
(b) It encouraged Indian industrial growth and political awarenes
(c) It weakened nationalist sentiments in Bengal
(d) It led to the immediate withdrawal of the British from India

(v) The extract mentions the suspension of the Non-Cooperation Movement after violent incidents in 192
Which of the following principles guided Gandhi's decision to suspend the movement? **(Application)** (

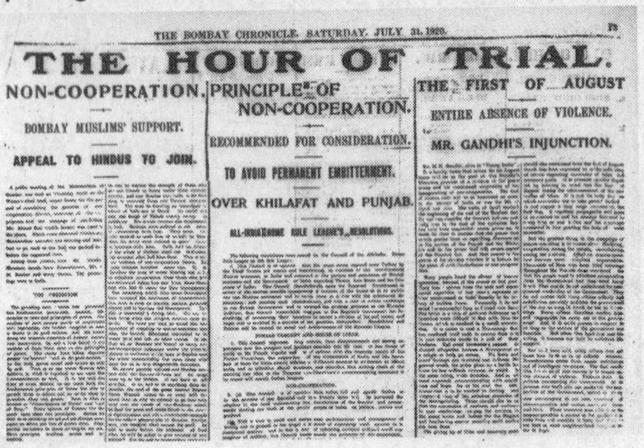
THE BOMBAY CHRONICLE, SATURDAY, JULY 31, 1920.

THE HOUR OF TRIAL.

NON-COOPERATION.

BOMBAY MUSLIMS' SUPPORT.

APPEAL TO HINDUS TO JOIN.

PRINCIPLE OF NON-COOPERATION.

RECOMMENDED FOR CONSIDERATION.

TO AVOID PERMANENT EMBITTERMENT.

OVER KHILAFAT AND PUNJAB.

THE FIRST OF AUGUST

ENTIRE ABSENCE OF VIOLENCE.

MR. GANDHI'S INJUNCTION.

Source: The Indian Expres

(P) Commitment to non-violence
(Q) Avoiding further loss of life
(R) Demanding immediate independence
(S) Strengthening Muslim-Hindu unity

(a) Only (P) and (Q) (b) Only (Q) and (R) (c) Only (P) and (R) (d) Only (R) and (S)

(vi) Given below are two statements marked Assertion and Reason. Read the statements carefully ar
choose the correct option. **(Understanding)** (

Assertion (A) The Lahore Session of Congress in 1929 declared Poorna Swaraj as the ultimate goal
the Indian National Congress.

Reason (R) The boycott of the Simon Commission and the failure of the Nehru Report led Congress
demand complete independence.

(a) Both Assertion and Reason are true and Reason is the correct explanation of Assertion.
(b) Both Assertion and Reason are true, but Reason is not the correct explanation of Assertion.
(c) Assertion is true and Reason is false.
(d) Both Assertion and Reason are false.

(vii) Which of the following events is most similar to the assassination of Archduke Franz Ferdinand in 19
as a trigger for a large-scale conflict? **(Application)** (

(a) The Boston Tea Party of 1773 that ignited the American Revolution
(b) The signing of the Treaty of Versailles in 1919
(c) The Congress of Vienna in 1815
(d) The formation of the League of Nations

(viii) Identify the key cause of the Wall Street Crash of 1929. **(Understanding) (1)**

(a) Excessive government regulation of banks and industries, which restricted economic growth and investor confidence.

(b) Speculative investments in the stock market combined with overproduction in industries, leading to a collapse of stock prices and widespread panic.

(c) Introduction of the New Deal policies by Roosevelt, which caused uncertainty in international trade and domestic markets.

(d) The outbreak of World War II disrupted international financial systems and stock exchanges.

(ix) The rise of militarism in Japan during the 1930s was mainly due to .... (Recall) **(1)**

(x) On 8th March 1917, women textile workers led a demonstration in Petrograd against food shortages and the war, which is often seen as the spark that ignited the wider revolt. *Source: History records* **(1)**

State any one political cause of the March Revolution. **(Recall)**

(xi) Expand IRI. **(Recall) (1)**

(xii) The image given below shows a portrait of a man giving a speech with a raised arm and the Nazi flag in the background. **(1)**

Source: historicalarchives.com

Name the leader shown in the image who became the Chancellor of Germany in 1933. **(Recall)**

(xiii) The image given below shows workers in a mill in Calcutta during the colonial period. **(1)**

Source: colonialindustryarchives.org

Refer to the image and name the major industry that developed in Bengal under British rule. **(Recall)**

(xiv) In the picture shown below, the social reformer .... can be seen encouraging people to reject caste discrimination and work towards social equality through the Satyashodhak Samaj. **(Recall) (1)**

Source: https://archives.vsktelangana.org/

(xv) In 1919, the British government passed the Rowlatt Act, which allowed the authorities to arrest and detain individuals without trial. This led to widespread protests across India and strong opposition from Indian leaders. **(1)**

What was the significance of the Rowlatt Act agitation in the growth of the Indian national movement? **(Understanding)**

(xvi) Mention any one reason for the boycott of the Simon Commission by the Indians in 1928. **(Recall) (1)**

Section - B

(32 Marks)

Question-2

With reference to the news extract given below, state any four ways in which British revenue policies affected peasants and artisans, leading to the disruption of the traditional economy. **(Understanding) (4)**

Calcutta Gazette

July 14, 1947

TRADITIONAL ECONOMY IN SHAMBLES

FOUR WAYS BRITISH REVENUE POLICIES RUINED RUINED PEASANTS AND ARTISANS

The relending extractied by British invenite policies, as nuted Spring tornar the current transfer of power, usen, has systematically decimated the very funudations of rural India.

(1) Exorbitant fixed cash revenue demands under systems like the Ryotwari forced peasant peasants into a viscoous in viscous cycle of debt, often often leading to total land alienation.

forced peasants into a viscous cycle of debt, often leading to total land alieration.

(2) This, in turn, fueled the monstrous growth of the moneylender class, who seized lands when high-interest debts could not be met, uprooting traditional tillers.

(3) Simultaneously, the flood of duty-free British manufactured particularly textiles, stranghled

(3) Simultaneously, the flood of duty-free British manufactured goods, particularly strangled stangled India's once-thriving artisan class, forcing millions out of work.

(4) The deliberate push for commercial crops, like indigo and opium for export, replacing, replacing food grains, further exacerbated rural distress and vulnerability to famine.

These policies have left an indelible scar on the nation's fabric.

Question-3

Jyotirao Phule worked extensively for the education of lower-caste children, Narayan Guru promoted social equality in Kerala and Veerasalingam campaigned against caste discrimination in Andhra. **(4)**

In the above context analyse the impact of the efforts of these social reformers on the caste system and social equality in 19th-century India. **(Analysis)**

Question-4

In 1899, the Munda tribe in Chotanagpur revolted against the British-imposed land revenue system and the exploitative zamindari system.

Source: The Indian Express **(4)**

Based on the above report, state any four circumstances that led to the Munda Uprising. **(Recall)**

Question-5

(i) How did the Partition of Bengal in 1905 lead to the emergence of the Swadeshi and Boycott Movements in India? **(Understanding) (4)**

Or

(ii) State any four causes that prompted the Indian people to launch the Swadeshi Movement against the Partition of Bengal. **(Understanding)**

Question-6

How did the implementation of the Rowlatt Act and the events at Jallianwala Bagh in 1919 influence the growth of mass nationalist movements in India? **(Analysis) (4)**

Question-7

The image given below shows Gandhi leading the Salt March during the Civil Disobedience Movement. Study the cartoon carefully and answer the questions that follow. **(4)**

Source: The Hindu

(i) Explain any two key features of the Civil Disobedience Movement that mobilised Indians across the country.

(ii) Discuss any two significant outcomes of the Gandhi-Irwin Pact and the resumption of the movement.

Question-8

State any two causes that led to the Wall Street Crash of 1929. Mention any two impacts of the Great Depression on the economies of the USA, Germany and Japan. **(Understanding) (4)**

Question-9

(i) The image given below shows the signing ceremony of the Treaty of Versailles. Identify the place where the treaty was signed and discuss any two criticisms of the Treaty of Versailles that explain why it failed to ensure lasting peace. **(Understanding) (4)**

Source: The Guardian

Or

(ii)

Discuss any four ways in which long-term causes like militarism, imperialism, nationalism and the alliance system contributed to the outbreak of World War I. **(Understanding)**

Section - C

(32 Marks)

Question-10

(i) On 8th March, 1917, workers and soldiers in Petrograd went on strike, demanding bread and an end to autocratic rule.

Source : hindu.com (8

(a) Identify the revolution being referred to. State any three immediate resu of the March Revolution. **(Recall**

(b) Discuss any four weaknesses of the Provisional Government that led to the November Revolution. **(Understanding**

Or

(ii) The New Economic Policy (NEP) introduced by Lenin in 1921 allowed limited private trade and smal businesses.

(a) In the light of the above statement, enumerate any four main features of the NEP. **(Recall**

(b) Elucidate any four impacts of the NEP on the Russian economy and society. **(Understanding**

Question-11

According to historian Mark Mazower, "Fascism in Italy rose out of post-war discontent and the fear of socialism." (8

In the context of the above statement, analyse the events that brought Benito Mussolini to power betwee 1919 and 1922. **(Understanding**

Question-12

In the period from 1932 to January 1933, Hitler emerged as the Chancellor of Germany amidst politica instability and economic crisis. **(Recal**

(i) In this context, discuss any four events that led to Hitler becoming the Chancellor of Germany. (

(ii) Analyse any four factors that assisted Hitler's rise and contributed to his popularity among differer groups in Germany. **(Recall)** (

Question-13

(i) Father of the Nation, Mahatma Gandhi, was the foremost leader of India's freedom movement. Gandh led the Indian independence movement from 1919 to 1947, and this period is known as Gandhi era Gandhiji was born on 2nd October, 1869, in Porbandar, Gujarat. Father Karamchand Gandhi was th Diwan of Rajkot.

Source: All Research Journal

With reference to the above source, analyse the role of Gandhian movements from 1927 to 1937 consolidating mass nationalism in India. **(Understanding)** (

Or

(ii) Gandhi addressing a crowd during the Salt March, 1930: "We shall break the salt laws without violence

With reference to the above source, answer the following.

(a) State any four key features of the Civil Disobedience Movement. **(Recall)** (

(b) Discuss any two consequences of the Civil Disobedience Movement for the Indian freedom strugg and for the British government. **(Understanding)** (

Answers

1. (i) (b) Railways

(ii) (a) Narayan Guru

(iii) (c) Munda Uprising

(iv) (b) It encouraged Indian industrial growth and political awareness

(v) (a) Only (P) and (Q)

(vi) (a) Both Assertion and Reason are true and Reason is the correct explanation of Assertion.

(vii) (a) The Boston Tea Party of 1773 that ignited the American Revolution

(viii) (b) Speculative investments in the stock market combined with overproduction in industries, leading to a collapse of stock prices and widespread panic.

(ix) Economic instability

(x) One political cause of the March Revolution was the autocratic rule of Tsar Nicholas II and the widespread dissatisfaction with the monarchy.

(xi) Institute for Industrial Reconstruction.

(xii) The leader shown in the image is Adolf Hitler, who became the Chancellor of Germany in 1933.

(xiii) The Jute Industry developed as a major industry in Bengal under British rule.

(xiv) Jyotirao Phule.

(xv) The significance of the Rowlatt Act agitation in the growth of the Indian national movement was that it marked the beginning of the first nationwide mass protest led by Mahatma Gandhi using the method of Satyagraha against British rule.

(xvi) One reason for the boycott of the Simon Commission by the Indians in 1928 was that the Commission had no Indian members and consisted entirely of British officials.

2. Four ways in which British revenue policies affected peasants and artisans, leading to the disruption of the traditional economy, were

- **Heavy Taxation on Peasants** The introduction of systems like Permanent Settlement and the Ryotwari system imposed high land revenue, leaving peasants in debt and poverty.
- **Exploitation by Moneylenders** Due to inability to pay high taxes, peasants became dependent on moneylenders, which often led to loss of land and economic instability.
- **Decline of Artisan Industries** Traditional artisans faced competition from British-manufactured goods due to policies favouring imports from Britain, causing many local crafts to decline.
- **Disruption of Rural Economy** High taxation and commercialisation of agriculture encouraged cash crops instead of food crops, resulting in famine vulnerability and a collapse of self-sufficient village economies.

3. The impact of the efforts of these social reformers on the caste system and social equality in 19th century India were

- **Promotion of Education among Lower Castes** Jyotirao Phule established schools for children of lower castes, which helped in breaking the monopoly of upper castes over education and created awareness about social rights.

- **Challenge to Caste-Based Discrimination** Narayan Guru, through his teachings and social reforms in Kerala, promoted the idea that all humans are equal, challenging the rigid caste hierarchy and reducing untouchability practices.
- **Social Reform in Andhra Region** Veerasalingam campaigned against caste restrictions in marriage, widow remarriage, and social practices, thereby encouraging social mobility and equality among marginalised communities.
- **Long-Term Social Impact** Collectively, these reformers weakened the traditional caste system, promoted secular and rational values, and laid the foundation for modern social reform movements in India.

4. Four circumstances that led to the Munda Uprising were

- **British Land Revenue System** The introduction of the Zamindari system disrupted traditional tribal land ownership, as Mundas were forced to pay high taxes to landlords and the colonial administration.
- **Exploitation by Zamindars** Tribal peasants were subjected to high rents and forced labour by zamindars, which caused widespread resentment among the Munda community.
- **Loss of Traditional Rights** Mundas lost their customary rights over land, forests and natural resources due to British legal interference and new land laws.
- **Economic Hardship and Social Distress** High taxation, forced labour, and loss of land led to poverty, starvation and social unrest, prompting the Mundas to revolt.

5. *(i)* The Partition of Bengal in 1905 led to the emergence of the Swadeshi and Boycott Movements in India in the following ways

- **Communal Division by the British** The British divided Bengal into Muslim-majority East Bengal and Hindu-majority West Bengal, creating religious tensions. This was seen as an attempt to weaken the nationalist movement by dividing communities.
- **Rise of Nationalist Sentiment** The partition sparked widespread anger and resentment among Indians, particularly the educated middle class and political leaders, who viewed it as an attack on Indian unity.
- **Emergence of the Swadeshi Movement** In response, Indians promoted Swadeshi, i.e., the use of Indian-made goods, to economically resist British authority and assert self-reliance.
- **Launch of Boycott Campaigns** Alongside Swadeshi, Indians boycotted British goods and institutions, refusing to cooperate with the colonial government, which marked the beginning of organised mass protest in India.

Or *(ii)* Four causes that prompted the Indian people to launch the Swadeshi Movement against the Partition of Bengal were as follows

- **Partition of Bengal by the British** The division of Bengal into East Bengal (Muslim-majority) and West Bengal (Hindu-majority) was seen as a deliberate strategy to divide and weaken Indian unity, which angered people across the country.

- ***Rise of Nationalist Sentiment*** *The educated middle class and political leaders felt the partition was an attack on Indian identity and culture, fueling nationalist feelings and the desire to resist colonial rule.*
- ***Economic Exploitation*** *The British aimed to increase dependence on British goods, which threatened Indian industries and artisans, motivating people to promote indigenous products (Swadeshi).*
- ***Mobilisation by Political Leaders*** *Leaders like Bal Gangadhar Tilak, Bipin Chandra Pal and Lala Lajpat Rai actively encouraged mass protests, boycotts and demonstrations, which helped unite people against the colonial decision.*

6. *The implementation of the Rowlatt Act and the events at Jallianwala Bagh in 1919 influenced the growth of mass nationalist movements in India in the following ways*

- ***Repressive Nature of the Rowlatt Act*** *The Act allowed the British government to arrest and detain political activists without trial, which angered Indians and was seen as a direct attack on civil liberties.*
- ***Widespread Protests and Satyagraha*** *Gandhi launched a satyagraha against the Rowlatt Act, mobilising students, peasants and urban workers across the country. This marked the beginning of mass political participation in India.*
- ***Jallianwala Bagh Massacre (13th April, 1919)*** *The firing on unarmed civilians in Amritsar, including women and children, shocked the nation and intensified anti-British sentiment, turning moderate opinion against colonial rule.*
- ***Growth of Nationalist Sentiment*** *The combination of repression and violence radicalised public opinion, strengthened the Indian National Congress, and paved the way for future nationwide movements like the Non-Cooperation Movement.*

7. (i) *Two key features of the Civil Disobedience Movement that mobilised Indians across the country were*

- ***Non-violent Protest and Mass Participation*** *Gandhi emphasised satyagraha (non-violent resistance), encouraging people across villages, towns and cities to refuse to obey unjust laws like the salt tax.*
- ***Boycott of British Goods and Institutions*** *Indians were encouraged to use indigenous goods, refuse to pay taxes, and resign from government jobs, which economically and politically challenged British authority and united diverse sections of society.*

(ii) *Two significant outcomes of the Gandhi-Irwin Pact and the resumption of the movement are*

- ***Partial Concessions by the British*** *The pact allowed freedom to make salt for personal use, release of political prisoners and withdrawal of ordinances against protesters, showing that mass movements could pressure the British government into negotiation.*
- ***Strengthening of National Unity and Political Awareness*** *The resumption of the movement after minor disagreements kept the momentum of mass political mobilisation alive, spreading political consciousness across rural and urban India and laying the groundwork for future struggles for complete independence.*

8. Two causes that led to the Wall Street Crash of 1929 were as follows

- **Over-speculation in the Stock Market** Investors bought shares on credit (buying on margin), causing artificially high stock prices that were unsustainable.
- **Weaknesses in Banking and Industry** Banks invested heavily in the stock market and industries faced overproduction with falling demand, creating economic instability.

Two impacts of the Great Depression on the economies of the USA, Germany and Japan were

- **Economic Collapse and Unemployment** In the USA, millions lost jobs; in Germany, industrial output fell sharply and in Japan, exports declined, leading to widespread unemployment and poverty.
- **Political and Social Unrest** The economic crisis strengthened extremist movements, such as Nazism in Germany, militarism in Japan, and social protests in the USA, influencing both domestic and international politics.

9. (i) The Treaty of Versailles was signed in Versailles, France.

The Treaty of Versailles failed to ensure lasting peace for the following reasons

- **Harsh Treatment of Germany** The treaty imposed heavy reparations, territorial losses, disarmament, and the war guilt clause, which created economic hardship and resentment in Germany.
- **Failure to Address National and Ethnic Realities** The new borders and creation of new states ignored cultural and ethnic considerations, leading to political instability and minority conflicts in Europe.

Or (ii) Four ways in which long-term causes like militarism, imperialism, nationalism and the alliance system contributed to the outbreak of World War I in the following ways

- **Militarism (Arms Race)** European powers, especially Germany and Britain, built large armies and navies in a competitive arms race, creating an atmosphere of suspicion and readiness for war.
- **Alliance System** Countries formed alliances like the Triple Alliance (Germany, Austria-Hungary, Italy) and Triple Entente (Britain, France, Russia). This meant that a conflict involving one country could rapidly escalate into a continent-wide war.
- **Imperialism** European nations competed fiercely for colonies and overseas territories, particularly in Africa and Asia, which increased rivalries and tensions between them.
- **Nationalism** Intense national pride and the desire for independence among ethnic groups (e.g., Serbs in the Balkans) encouraged confrontations and fueled political instability.

10. (i) (a) The revolution being referred to is the March Revolution of 1917 in Russia.

Three immediate results of the March Revolution were

- **Abdication of Tsar Nicholas II** The revolution forced the last Russian emperor to abdicate, ending over three centuries of Romanov rule.
- **Formation of the Provisional Government** A temporary government was established, led by liberal politicians and members of the Duma, to run the country until a constituent assembly could be elected.